JOHN DUNS SCOTUS'

POLITICAL AND ECONOMIC PHILOSOPHY

JOHN DUNS SCOTUS'

POLITICAL AND ECONOMIC PHILOSOPHY

LATIN TEXT AND ENGLISH TRANSLATION

With an Introduction and Notes

By

Allan B. Wolter, O.F.M.

The Franciscan Institute
St. Bonaventure, New York
2001

© The Franciscan Institute
St. Bonaventure University
St. Bonaventure, New York
2001

Text Series No. 24

Library of Congress Card Number: 2001095787

ISBN: 1-57659-172-7

Printed in the United States of America
BookMasters
Mansfield, Ohio

TABLE OF CONTENTS

PREFACE

In my source book of texts and translations entitled *Duns Scotus on the Will and Morality*, I noted that unlike Thomas Aquinas, Scotus never commented on Aristotle's *Politics* nor did he write any significant political tracts like Ockham. Nevertheless, despite his primary philosophical reputation as a metaphysician, Scotus did have certain definitive ideas about both politics and the morality of the marketplace. In the Introduction to my work I called attention to the question in Bk. IV of his *Ordinatio* (dist. 15, q. 2) and the parallel account in the report of his Paris lectures on this distinction (qq. 2-4) as containing "the most extensive statement of his 'political and economic philosophy." Because of the nature and purpose of my book, however, I was able to include only a few pages from the *Ordinatio* question under the heading of "Positive Law and Civil Authority," for his ideas on the origin of the state and the source of political jurisdiction seemed surprisingly modern. However, the question in which this item occurs is found in Scotus' treatise of sacramental theology and is ostensibly about whether restitution is required for licitly receiving the sacrament of penance. Most of this unusually lengthy question is devoted to showing how an individual person legitimately acquires ownership or the right to use property, and the origin of civil authority enters in even more peripherally because distinct ownership of material things according to Augustine and the canonists stems from positive law. In fact the entire question is somewhat of a surprise, for who would expect even a "subtle doctor" to dig so far back to discover the philosophical roots of a penitent's obligation to make restitution for ill-gotten gains?

One hypothesis for his doing so that initially suggested itself to me was this—a master of any caliber during his regency at Paris would be expected to conduct at least one public *Quodlibet* for the theological faculty. In such a disputation, as the name implies, *any* question on *any* topic of current theological interest by *any* member present, be he a master, bachelor or only an interested spectator had to be fielded by the master chairing the disputation. With an eye to such a future test of their theological expertise, magisterial aspirants, especially among the late scholastics, often introduced a relatively short but highly systematic treatment of some important theological topic in a most unexpected place. This seemed to be to be especially true of Scotus' *Ordinatio*, or final version of his *Commentary on the Sentences*, prepared for public distribution. Who of us, for example, would expect him to be treating a

subject like slavery under the sacrament of marriage? Why be surprised, then, if he dealt with the origin of the state or the ethics of the marketplace under the sacrament of penance?

But a more interesting suggestion came to mind when I reflected that we have no direct evidence that Scotus ever commented on Bk. IV of the *Sentences* at Oxford. We have no *lectura* from this period and the portion originally published under the title of the *Opus oxoniense* or Oxford Commentary contains a reference in distinction 25, question 1, to a bull of Pope Benedict XI that Scotus saw with his own eyes, something that could only have occurred after the momentous events that occurred at the close of his first year in Paris and the death of Pope Boniface VIII as the result of his imprisonment by Nogaret, the minister of Philip the Fair. What brought the long-standing feud between the French king and Boniface VIII to its unhappy climax was precisely the question of whether Philip as a Christian king owed his feudal possessions and his political authority to the pope as the Vicar of Christ. Such was the claim of the papal absolutist, Master Giles of Rome, who some twenty years earlier had tutored young Philip. The extreme interpretation of the plenitude of papal power in his mature work *De ecclesiastica potestate* went far beyond Boniface's *Ausculta fili* (December 1301) that the king's minister, Pierre Flotte took such pains to misrepresent to the first session of the French Estates-General (April 1302).

Perhaps no topic was more hotly discussed when Scotus first crossed the channel later that year than the origin of temporal possessions and the source of political authority, not only in university circles by theologians like the two Augustinian friars Giles of Rome or his disciple, James of Viterbo, but by the French Parliament and the common man in the street. If Scotus composed this portion of the *Ordinatio* after his return to Paris during the papacy of Benedict XI, perhaps our wonder should be, not that he went so deeply into the source of *dominium* and political authority, but that he treated such topics, presumably of little interest to a follower of the "Poor Man of Assisi," so extensively and yet so prudently.

Since it will be some years before the Scotus Commission preparing the critical Vatican edition makes this important question available for students, I have prepared a Latin text based on a reading of two of the best manuscripts for Bk. IV of the *Ordinatio*. Both have a wealth of critical marginal notes and are described by Carl Balic in his "De Ordinatione I. Duns Scoti disquisitio historico-critica," that serves as the editorial introduction to *Ioannis Duns Scoti Opera Omnia*, tom. I (Civitas Vaticana: Typis Polyglottis Vaticanis, 1950), pp. 12*-28*, 32*-

34*. The first MS, known as Codex A, from the city library in Assisi (cod. 137), is an early 14th century attempt at a critical edition of Scotus' unfinished *Ordinatio*, and is the primary source or *editio princeps* of the Vatican version. Our question is found on fols. 233ra-235va. The second is Codex M (Merton College, Oxford, cod. 66) that contains the text of Bk. I and Bk. IV of the *Ordinatio*. Our question is contained in fol. 192va-195vb. Codex M is written in a semicursive style in several hands. A second hand has carefully corrected the work of the original scribe inserting what he omitted and clarifying his ambiguous or incorrect abbreviations. The difference between Codices M and A is minimal, however, consisting mainly of inversion of words or obvious homoeoteleuton omissions. The two MSS seem to have had independent access to a common source, however, rather than that either depended directly upon the other. We have examined two other MSS of Vienna, but as they are of inferior quality we have omitted collating them, only noting here they seemed to have nothing of importance to add to our text. One is the 14th century Codex Palatinus 1416, the other Codex Palatinus 1423 from the 15th century. In general we have kept the reading of Codex A as primary, resorting to M only to correct obvious omissions and paleographical doublets where the scribe was not sure of the original reading.

I am indebted to Fathers Gedeon Gal for suggestions regarding the Latin text and to Father William J. Haney for reading the Introduction. I am also grateful to F. Edward Coughlin, O.F.M., who did the layout, format, and design of this publication. As always I am extremely grateful to The Franciscan Institute and Margaret Carney, O.S.F., the Dean/Director in particular for her encouragement and support in the publication of this volume, which I first privately printed in 1989 in Old Mission Santa Barbara, CA.

The Franciscan Institute
St. Bonaventure, New York
December 8, 2000

INTRODUCTION

Harris in his two volume study of John Duns Scotus devotes considerable attention to the question we have edited here because he sees it as "a very interesting and complete statement of the theory of sovereignty and the social contract, not unlike that enunciated later by Hobbes, Locke, and Rousseau, and presented in such a way as to avoid some of the exaggeration of later writers."[1] After devoting a dozen pages to analyzing its contents he concludes with the observation "Such is the brief sketch Scotus gives of his political philosophy, and it is introduced only incidentally in a *quaestio* in which he is inquiring into the conditions which must be observed in making restitution for a wrong done. It is perhaps the only topic on which one might wish he had written at greater length. But the friar and the metaphysician had little interest in political matters. He gives us tantalizing glimpses of a new theory of the state which several centuries later was to influence so profoundly the politics of Europe, with no apparent consciousness of the importance of his theme. He sees the problem, outlines a solution, and passes on, without betraying any deep interest in a world which he had renounced. Yet in a few sentences he has stated very clearly the essential elements of a theory of human society which was to revolutionize not only the thought but the practice of the Western world, and it is to him that we can trace in a very real sense the beginnings of modern political science."[2]

If John Duns entered the Franciscan Order at a very early age, as seems to be the case, he might well be thought to have been shielded to some extent from the more mundane happenings of the world.[3] For in

---

[1] C. R. S. Harris, *John Duns Scotus*, vol. II (Oxford: Clarendon Press, 1927), p. 347.

[2] *Ibid.*, p. 357.

[3] The Scotist John (Mair) Major whose own home was only "seven or eight leagues" from that of John Duns, was likely to have been conversant with the history of the neighborhood and of John's entry into the Order. He reports that "when he was no more than a boy, but had been already grounded in grammar, he was taken by two Scottish Minorite friars to Oxford, for at that time there existed no university in Scotland. By the favor of those friars he lived in the convent of the Minorites at Oxford and made his profession in the religion of Blessed Francis." (*A History of Greater Britain as well England as Scotland Compiled from the Ancient Authorities by John Major, by name indeed a Scot, but by profession a Theologian*. Translated from the original Latin by Archibald Constable (Edinburgh, University Press, 1892), p. 206.) If, as seems to be the case, the Duns family

taking the Franciscan vow of poverty, he would according to the ideals of his Order have tried to "go through the world as a pilgrim and stranger."[4] But if, as a child of his time, Scotus' knowledge of economic matters might be somewhat limited,[5] he could hardly have been as naive or indifferent to political matters as Harris seems to believe.

King Alexander III of Scotland died in 1296 when John Duns was 21 and the powerful king of England, Edward I attempted to extend his suzerainty over Scotland, first in peaceful ways, but eventually initiating a bloody warfare between the two countries that continued long beyond the death of Scotus. During much of John's study years at Oxford, Edward was also at war with Philip IV of France. Neither was the university an ivory tower unaffected by the expansionistic claims of these two most powerful kings in the north of Europe, since neither students nor masters were free to cross the channel for academic pursuits. For when Philip[6] and his wily ministers[7] tricked the Edward

---

had relatives or close friends among the friars who recognized young John's precocity, it would more easily account not only for Scotus' being taken into a Franciscan friary as a "puer oblatus" or postulant even before he was of canonical age to become a novice, but also for his being taken to Oxford University rather than to some friary in Scotland.

[4] Most of the religious founders quote the passage from the Acts of the Apostles (4:32) about the early Christian community where property was shared in common and which inspired St. Augustine's account that Scotus refers to as the original state in which man was created. This implies that the natural "settled-in" state of mankind was to possess the goods of the earth in common. St. Francis of Assisi never quotes this passage in his Rule, however, and, where one would expect him to do so, cites instead I Peter (2:11). Franciscans are to regard themselves rather "as *strangers and pilgrims* in this world" so far as worldly possessions are concerned. [The Rule of 1223, ch. 6 in *St. Francis of Assisi: Writings and Early Biographies*, ed. M. A. Habig (Chicago: Franciscan Herald Press, 1973), p. 61].

[5] As Harris points out: "Of the operation of purely economic laws he is almost entirely ignorant, and he attempts, in accordance with the general practice of the Middle Ages, to regulate the conduct of the business world by an ethical code which rings strangely in modern ears." (*op. cit.*, p. 355)

[6] Historians are divided in their estimates of the complex character of this grandson of St. Louis XI. Was he a master of statecraft who brought the French monarchy to new heights of power or was he just a handsome figurehead manipulated by a group of clever but ambitious and unscrupulous lawyers, like Peter Flotte or William Nogaret, who served as Philip's ministers and always spoke for him on formal occasions? To Dante he was the "woe of France" and one French bishop characterized him as "pope, king and emperor in one person."

[7] Cantor gives this unflattering description of Philip's advisors: "The enormous power which the French monarchy enjoyed at the accession of Philip IV the Fair (1285–1314) had a corrupting effect on the personnel of the royal bureaucracy, especially the chief ministers of the crown. The vast resources which they controlled . . . and their

into a full scale war in 1294, he forbad all passages of ships to the continent from the British isles and wrote letters to every bishop, the provincials of the Dominicans and Franciscans, and the chancellor of the university of Oxford, explaining how he had been forced into war, and begged for prayers in every church in the land.[8]

If Scotus was at Oxford, as seems probable,[9] he may not yet have been fully aware of the even more serious politico-ecclesiastical feud that was brewing on the continent between Philip the Fair and Pope Boniface VIII.[10] Knowledge of that would come forcefully enough later.

---

almost unlimited power to ruin men born to a much higher social status made them into arrogant and unprincipled scoundrels. Since the time of Philip Augustus the French bureaucracy had been known for its harsh attitudes, and this was to some degree a political necessity if the country was ever to be really united under the crown. But the megalomania of Philip the Fair's ministers was something new. To severity and chicanery was now added slander, blackmail, and extortion. The government of thirteenth-century France discovered the technique of the 'big lie': the more fantastic the accusation the easier it would be to destroy helpless opponents. It learned how the processes of law could be easily perverted into an invincible agency of despotism. The royal administration always acted against its helpless victims with a parade of legal formalities; it discovered that if governments will only use a façade of juristic institutions, the most extreme and groundless accusations will begin to take on the coloration of truth in the dim minds of the populace. It is not easy to discern what part the king played in all this—to what extent he actually directed this vicious policy or was merely the dupe of his ministers. The latter is more probable. Personally devout and brave, Philip was also silent and stupid, the perfect façade behind which the bureaucracy could work its plans. His ministers were monsters of cynicism, but the king seems actually to have believed their big lies. They had no trouble convincing him of the legality of their attacks on anyone who stood in their way, including the vicar of Christ himself." (Norman M. Cantor, *Medieval History*, New York/London: Macmillan and Collier-Macmillan, 1963), pp. 561-62)

[8] Sir Maurice Powicke, *The Thirteenth Century 1216-1307*, Oxford: Clarendon Press, 1953, p. 648.

[9] It has been widely claimed that Scotus must have spent some time in Paris between 1291 and 1300. See A. Callebaut, "Le bx. Jean Duns Scot étudiant à Paris," in *Archivum Franciscanum Historicum* 17 (1924), pp. 3-12; É. Longpré, "Gonsalve de Balboa et le B. Duns Scot," *Études Franciscaines* 36 (1924), 640-45. This claim, however, has been plausibly challenged by C. K. Brampton, and the dates given for his Paris sojourn by Balic can hardly be correct. He would have had to go before the channel was closed to scholars by Edward I and he would have had to stay longer than the four year period claimed by Balic and could not possibly have fulfilled the theological requirements for participation as a "formed bachelor" in the dispute of Master Bridlington some time during the latter's regency at Oxford (1300-1301). See C. K. Brampton, "Duns Scotus at Oxford, 1288-1301), *Franciscan Studies* 24 (1964), 5-20.

[10] From his first accession to the papal throne on Christmas eve (1294) Boniface VIII in the interests of promoting another crusade as a common cause of Christian Europe quickly sought to impose peace on its warring feudal and city states, particularly since their rulers had begun heavily taxing the clergy for their respective military campaigns

He would, however, have been aware of the Pope's effort to impose peace on Europe's warring factions in the interest of uniting Christendom for a crusade. In particular, he must have appreciated Boniface's attempt to force Edward to make peace with his native Scotland.[11] Though Boniface's effort failed, the king realized he could not fight both the Scots and the French so he made peace with Philip.[12] Once more scholars could cross the channel for studies in Paris as Scotus must have done in time to begin the fall term of 1302.

When Scotus came to the French capital in the late summer or fall, he was confronted with the full details of the second dispute between

---

against one another. The Fourth Lateran Council (1215) forbad taxation of the clergy without the consent of the pope. Boniface, a canonist by profession, chose this as his weapon to stop these feudal disputes and commercial city rivalries. Using the threat of excommunication to bring peace to the various cities of Lombardy, Venice and Genoa, he applied the same the technique to England and France. Their two Christian kings claimed each was waging a "just war" against the other to justify the severe taxes they levied on the clergy. To end this intolerable situation, Boniface issued the Bull *Clericis laicos* (Feb. 1296). The bull could have been more diplomatically worded, for it began with the harsh accusation that "the laity have always been hostile to the clergy" and the recent taxations are another example of such. In the future, the Pope decreed, any ruler (king, emperor or civil authority), who demanded taxes of his clergy without the pope's previous permission incurs automatic excommunication as does any cleric who yields to such demands. The bull was bitterly resented by both Philip and Edward who more than any others had provoked it. The English king could only vent his anger against the primate Archbishop of Canterbury and his clergy by removing them from the protection of the common law. Philip found a more direct way of striking back at the Pope by cutting off the heavy revenues from the French clergy that the papacy needed for its financial support and he refused to honor any special liberties customarily granted the clergy. Pressured by the latter, the Pope adopted more conciliatory measures. His bull *Ineffabilis amor* (Sept. 20, 1296) explained that the pope had never intended to prevent taxation of the clergy when defense of the realm was at stake, and *Romana mater* (Feb. 7, 1297) permitted Philip to receive voluntary contributions of the clergy in times of pressing necessity. Six months later his *Etsi statu* (July 31) for all practical purposes nullified the *Clericis laicos* by permitting the king to judge for himself when national defense requires taxation of the clergy and waiving any necessity of getting papal approval for such. On their part, the two kings whose quarrel had precipitated the whole affair, submitted their causes to Boniface, who agreed to arbitrate between them in his private capacity as Benedict Caetani. So ended the first encounter between the French king and the Pope.

[11] Cf. Powicke, *The Thirteenth Century 1216-1307*, pp. 693, 702, 705-706.

[12] Edward signed an independent truce with Philip initially at Vyve-Saint-Bavon on the river Lys in October 9, 1297, and during the following year both Edward (in February) and Philip (in March) wrote to Boniface, who agreed to arbitrate between them. Philip, however, insisted he do so as a private person and not in his official capacity as pope. For the sake of peace, his primary intention, Boniface consented to this stipulation.

Boniface and Philip.[13] The national animosity, stirred up by the crudely forged bull *Deum time* and the events that followed,[14] was still running high. It was tempered somewhat, however, by concern over the humiliating defeat the French forces had suffered in Flanders along with the death of the king's chief minister Peter Flotte.[15]

But with the opening of the fall term in the first week of October, Scotus had to turn his full attention to academic affairs. On October 30, Boniface opened the promised council, and many of the French clergy

---

[13] The second and more serious conflict between Boniface and Philip broke out when the king arrested Bishop Saisset in 1301 as a traitor and tried and imprisoned him in open defiance of the jurisdiction of the pope over all bishops and their right to clerical immunity. Boniface in December angrily protested in the bull *Ausculta fili* "Listen son..." rebuking Philip for his abuse of clerical patronage that was subverting the whole state of the French church. Unfortunately it also contained the inflammatory remark: "Let no one persuade you that you have no superior or that you are not subject to the head of the ecclesiastical hierarchy, for he is a fool who so thinks..." Though the precise spiritual nature of this 'subjection' was not specified, Philip and his ministers seized upon this remark as the basis for their propaganda against the pope. The original bull was burned and a crude substitute (*Deum time*) was circulated containing the words "Fear God and keep his commandments. We want you to know you are subject to us in spiritualities and in temporalities..." To this the king was reputed to have replied: "Philip, by the grace of God king of the French, to Boniface who acts as though he were pope, little or no greeting. Let your great fatuity know that in temporalities we are subject to no one..." For a good account of the dispute accompanied by selected documents, see Brian Tierney, *The Crisis of Church and State 1050-1300* (Englewood Cliffs, NJ: Prentice-Hall, 1964.), pp. 173-210; more detail can be found in T. S. R. Boase, *Boniface VIII* (London: Constable and Co, 1933), pp. 297-337; for a shorter assessment of Boniface's position see Sir Maurice Powicke, "Pope Boniface VIII" in *The Christian Life in the Middle Ages and Other Essays* (Oxford: Clarendon Press, 1935), pp. 48-73.

[14] In his original bull, *Ausculta fili*, the Pope had summoned the French archbishops, bishops, the masters of theology and canon law, and other ecclesiastics to come to Rome for a council to begin on November 1 of the following year. Philip, however, forbad his clergy to attend such and, to mobilize national opinion in his favor, he countered by calling his own assembly of nobles, clergy and bourgeoisie. At this first meeting of the Estates-General in April 10, 1302, Peter Flotte had accused Boniface of claiming to be feudal overlord of France. When the pope first heard the report of this from the French envoys in June, he angrily replied that as canon lawyer with 40 years experience, he had never made such a preposterous claim, but that his predecessors had deposed three French kings and he was quite prepared to do the same with Philip if necessary.

[15] There was a summer lull in the storm, when Philip's forces suffered a disastrous defeat by the Flemings at the battle of Courtrai July 11, 1302, where Flotte was among the slain. Boniface was quickly informed of the defeat, and thus was encouraged in his opposition to Philip and his determination to defend the unity of the Church which he saw seriously challenged when bishops were forced to choose between submission to their national ruler and obedience to the pope. For details see Powicke, "Pope Boniface VIII," p. 70; Boase, *op. cit.*, p. 312.

defying the king's prohibition left Paris to attend,[16] but little was accomplished toward easing the Church/State tensions in France.[17] More drastic measures were needed, and immediately after its close, Boniface began drafting his *Unam sanctam*, the most famous medieval document on the spiritual and temporal power of the Church.[18]

---

[16] Less than half of the 78 French bishops summoned, attended the council. Many of these were sympathetic towards the king, if not towards his ministers, and were opposed to any extreme measures against the crown. For details of the council see Boase, *op. cit*, pp. 316-17.

[17] As one chronicler put it: "There was much talk but not much done." Peter Flotte's memory was condemned and his family and relatives deprived of all their ecclesiastical dignities, but Philip was not formally censured. As Boase notes, the council probably was over on November 18 when a bull was drawn up excommunicating all who prevented the faithful from access to Rome. (*Ibid.*, p. 317)

[18] As Brian Tierney notes: "The bull was essentially a theological treatise on the unity of the Church . . . But it also emphasized, perhaps more explicitly than any earlier papal pronouncement, the power of the pope to 'institute' and to judge temporal kings." (B. Tierney, "Boniface VIII, Pope," *New Catholic Encyclopedia*, vol. 2, p. 672.) Sir Maurice Powicke sets the bull in historical perspective when he writes: "Pope Boniface VIII may have been unwise in his choice of the occasion of his great pronouncements, but he was no revolutionary seeking after an unfamiliar world. The famous bull *Unam sanctam* is one of the most carefully drafted documents which have ever emerged from the papal chancery. It is a formal exposition of the plenitude of papal power, spiritual and temporal, and was later included in the *Extravagantes communes*, a collection of decretals made at the end of the fifteenth century, which became part of the *Corpus Iuris Canonici*. In its emphasis upon the derivative nature of secular power—that, while part of the divine order, this has a dependent, not an independent authority—it follows the argument of Giles of Rome, the foremost apologist of the papacy. Two of its main theses are derived, through Giles and other writers, from a famous passage in Hugh of St. Victor and the equally famous, though much discussed treatment, by St. Bernard of the doctrine of the two swords. In the same year, 1302, in which the bull was issued, the same high claims were admitted in formal terms by the chancellor of Albert of Austria, the emperor-elect. Anti-papal propaganda, especially in France, had provoked Boniface. But drastic doctrine in politics had often, perhaps always been made possible by opposition . . . The point is that in the eyes of the papalists who looked over Europe about the year 1300, the position of *Unam sanctam*, if the precious heritage from the past was to be maintained, was the only position to take, and if, logic was to be the order of the day, had its rational and natural roots in the experience of the Church" ("Pope Boniface VIII," pp. 54-55). Boase adds this comment on its style. "Among Boniface's bulls it has a distinctive position. It is for him curiously impersonal. . . The whole form and wording of it is as of a general statement detached from any particular circumstances: even the French are nowhere specifically mentioned, and the opponents of the power of the Holy See are merely described as 'the Greeks and others who pretend that they are not subject to Peter and his successors.' As has repeatedly been pointed out, it contains little new. It is a careful statement of the claims of the papacy to final sovereignty, and bases the claim on the divine origin of that power, not on any practical necessities, nor even historical precedents, for there is no mention of the transference of the empire or the deposition of the last Merovingian. It is

In Paris its promulgation triggered the crown's violent and brutal attack on the Pope's reputation and person that would affect the whole city including the university campus and the Franciscan convent where Scotus as a bachelor of theology had begun his lectures on the *Sentences*.[19] The troubles that would close the university and lead to the exile of most of the foreign born students and masters, began on March 7, 1303 when Philip's new minister, William Nogaret[20] was invested with full power to act in the royal interests. Five days later Philip called a council of his chief advisers at the Louvre and Nogaret outlined the crowns' official policy for removing any threat from Boniface, for if one

---

as an 'order established by God' that it must be obeyed: it is a power formally revealed by Christ to St. Peter, and as such is an article of faith, necessary for salvation. This is the primary case for the papal power; it had often been stated before and the bull's greatest novelty is its absence of involved proof. Amid the controversial literature of the period it sounds a note of solemn and eloquent certainty. Of the views of theorists of the time Boniface in fact avails himself little: he borrows phrases from them; it is clear that some at least he has read; but he does not incorporate their conclusions" (*op. cit*, pp. 318-19). As Powicke notes, it contains echoes of the thinking of Giles of Rome. Historians commonly claim this prominent and influential writer, former tutor to young prince Philip and present Archbishop of Brouges, at least 'inspired' the *Unam sanctam* by his *De ecclesiastica potestate*, if he did not actually ghost-write it. But as Boase points out, Giles puts out a much more extreme view of papal supremacy than Boniface ever expressed. "In *Unam sanctam* we find only a solemn statement, on the grounds of revealed faith, of the supremacy of the spiritual power, and it would be quite possible to accept the comparatively moderate view of the manner in which that supremacy was exercised" (*Ibid.*, p. 319). James of Viterbo, Giles' successor to the Augustinian chair of theology in Paris, held similar but somewhat more tempered views than Giles' on the origin of political authority and property rights, and, as Boase notes, "definitely produced his treatise *De regimine christiano* as a contribution to the disputes of 1302" (*Ibid.*, p. 320).

[19] For a detailed account of the events that surrounded this last chapter in the conflict between Philip and Boniface, see Boase, *op. cit.*, pp. 315-337; Powicke, *art. cit*, pp. 41-73; Tierney, *The Crisis of Church and State 1050-1300*, pp. 180-92; R. A. Newhall, "The Affair at Anagni," *Catholic Historical Review* 1 (1921), 277-295.

[20] A native of Toulouse, and former professor of Law at Montpellier, Nogaret was even more anti-clerical than Flotte. There is some evidence that his parents may have been burned as heretics. Sir Maurice describes him graphically as coming "from a land full of bitter memories. He belonged to a people whose sceptical but passionate, outlook had no room for the tenacious orthodoxy and disciplined tradition which made compromise with its relations with the Church almost a matter of principle at the French court. Nogaret was a clerk in minor orders, *magister* as well as *miles regis*; he could quote Scripture and St. Augustine with the facility of a schoolman; he professed at every turn to be serving the true interests of the Church; and he had a very definite idea of the part which the king of France, the eldest son of the Church, should play. He was more obstinate than Boniface himself, and he was carried along by a cold fury more sinister and dreadful than Boniface's hot passion" (Powicke, *op. cit.*, pp. 70-71).

could prove he was no legitimate pope, a 'Bonifacius by name, but a Maleficus by deed,' his excommunications meant nothing. As Sir Maurice describes the accusations Nogaret offered to present to a council of the Church:[21] "Boniface was a false prophet, a heretic[22] and a man of evil life, who had not entered the sheepfold by the door, but had climbed in by another way. In the interests of the Church, and to avoid schism, the Pope must be secured and a faithful shepherd of the sheep appointed. The king of France, following the footsteps of his ancestors, must come to the aid of our mother, the Roman Church, and strike her fetters from her."

Theologians like John (Quidort) of Paris, the famous Dominican preacher, had pointed out that just as the pope might excommunicate an unworthy king and release his subjects from any moral obligation to obey him, so the king might also take steps to encourage the college of cardinals who had appointed the pope or a general council of the Church to judge whether an unworthy occupant of the chair of Peter should be replaced. For if a pope through the abuse of the spiritual sword, such as pronouncing anyone a heretic who denied the king of France was subject to him, had created danger of rebellion, the king might defend himself and his country by using his influence to bring about the pope's excommunication and deposition.[23]

Philip, with this in mind, on March 24 sent out letters appealing for a general council in the hope of enlisting other Christian princes for his cause. On April 30 Boniface countered by promulgating the *Patris aeterni* accepting Albert of Hapsburg as lawful emperor, and as such the immediate overlord of the King of the Franks. A month later he urged

---

[21] Powicke, *art. cit.*, p. 70.

[22] The main charge of heresy, on the grounds of which a pope, since he was no longer a member of the Church, could be deposed, seems to have been Boniface's reputed claim that regal power comes from God through the mediacy of the papacy. Earlier the legitimacy of Celestine V's resignation and Boniface's election to the papacy had been challenged on the grounds that a pope, once elected could not resign. Giles of Rome, former tutor to the King himself, and now the "doctor communis" of the Augustinian Order, had ably defended the pope's right to resign, so this was no longer an issue at Paris. Other charges as to how Boniface had criminally engineered his own election were devised by the king's lawyers and the two Colonna cardinals Boniface had deposed in connection with a robbery of a convoy of papal funds being brought to Rome from the pope's palace in Anagni.

[23] Cf. J. A. Watt, *John of Paris: On Regal and Papal Power* (Toronto: The Pontifical Institute of Mediaeval Studies, 1971), p. 57.

all subjects of the empire to throw off any allegiance to France. Nogaret evidently persuaded Philip that diplomatic measures against Boniface were useless and military force must be used. Philip, to free himself from any other enmities, abandoned any claim to Gascony and made final peace with England (May 20) and took other political steps to strengthen his position. One that would affect Scotus directly was his decision to marshal public opinion of his own country behind him.

On June 13 he summoned a full two-day meeting of his council. Five archbishops, twenty-one bishops, eleven abbots represented the higher clergy. At the first session a resolution was introduced demanding a legitimate pope to replace Boniface and begging Philip as a defender of the faith to summon a general Church council to replace him.[24] On the following day an indictment under twenty-nine heads was brought against Boniface.[25] Ten days later, on the feast of John the Baptist (June 24), the king organized an outdoor rally to publicize the results. The clergy and religious paraded through the Paris streets to the garden of the Louvre. There Bertold of St. Denys, bishop of Orleans and ex-chancellor of the university, together with two Franciscans and two Dominicans addressed the meeting.[26] The following day the king's commissioners interviewed each friar at the Franciscan house of studies to determine whether he would back the king's effort to remove the heretical pope who claimed power over the kingdom of France. Apart from the French who were more easily

---

[24] Nogaret, before leaving for Italy in May, seems to have arranged for several of the French nobles, to formally present the resolution to the council, and for William of Plaisans, one of the king's lawyers, as their spokesman to read the cause for indictment.

[25] As Boase (*op. cit.*, p. 333) describes it: "It was a strange and ingenious mixture of true and sordid imaginings. Incidents have been seized upon and distorted; angry exclamations, only too easily secured, have been transformed into professions of faith or declarations of policy . . . The deserved criticism that underlies much of it is completely invalidated by its fantastic exaggerations; it is invective, not evidence . . . It was now Boniface the man, that Benedict Caetani, whom France was always so ready to detach from his office; but behind their fear and hatred was the deeper design of prejudicing the Holy See through the reviling of its occupant. The excess of vituperation appears to-day as a hopeless confession of a weak case" (Boase, *ibid.* p. 334). It is clear why the majority of students and masters, not blinded by a fanatical loyalty to France or pressured by the crown, saw this vicious and unprecedented attack on the person of the pope for what it really was. Like Scotus and Gonsalvus of Spain, they chose exile or arrest to signing their approval to such an unheard of attack on the papacy, one that Philip and his ministers would continue to pursue even after they had literally hounded their enemy to death.

[26] A. J. Little, in "Chronological Notes on the Life of Scotus," *English Historical Review* 47 (1932), p. 575-76.

persuaded by the anti-papal propaganda, only three or four graduate students from across the channel or from Italy, signed the notarized statement that the Friars Minor of Paris assembled in chapter endorsed King Philip's appeal to a general council and a future true and lawful pope against Boniface VIII.[27] Two listings of the eighty some who refused to sign include the names of Scotus and Gonsalvus of Spain, the regent master of the Franciscans.[28] The penalty for this dissent was exile from the realm of France within three days.

Did Scotus spend his exile in England, still at war with Scotland, or somewhere on the continent as Gonsalvus,[29] his master did? If he went to Bologna as has been suggested, he may have learned more quickly of the events that followed. If he returned to Oxford, in the diocese of Lincoln, he would have learned something from the Bishop Dalderby who kept informed through his representative at Anagni where Boniface spent the summer at his ancestral palace. It was early August, however, before the full news from France reached Boniface. In a bull dated August 15, 1303, he suspended the right of the University of Paris to grant the degree of master of theology and canon and civil law.[30] Nogaret meanwhile had arrived in Italy to consult with Philip's friends and Boniface's enemies as to how to force his resignation.[31] He set up headquarters at the castle of Staggia, near Sienna, that belonged to Philip's Italian financier. From there he gathered a band of mercenaries,

---

[27] A day after the Franciscans the Dominicans were interviewed in similar fashion and 132, mostly French with a few foreign born, acceded to the king's demands. *Ibid.*, p. 575.

[28] These lists, discovered by Longpré in the Archives Nationales at Paris, are discussed by Little, *op. cit.*, p. 576.

[29] Gonsalvus would become the next Minister General of the Franciscan Order the following year and in that capacity appoint Scotus to be the next occupant of the Franciscan chair of theology at Paris.

[30] Little, *op. cit.*, p. 577.

[31] Historians are divided as to the precise nature of Nogaret's commission from his king. He only admitted having instructions to consult with Philip's Italian friends about the threatened unity of the church and inform the Pope about the French demands for a council, but he denied having a royal commission to employ troops. Philip, however, would hardly have compromised his position openly even if he were the prime mover of the attack on the pope. (see note 6 above). As Beck notes: "The attack of September 7 bears all the evidence of hasty planning; it was gotten up within five or six days. It sprang not so much from careful planning, as from the sudden realization of what Boniface was about at Anagni and that unless he were stymied by September 8, he would publish to the world his excommunication of the French monarch" (Henry G. J. Beck, "William Hundleby's Account of the Anagni Outrage," *Catholic Historical Review* 22 [1947], p. 209).

enlisting re-enforcements from discontented nobles in the Campagna and enemies of the Caetani family, like the Colonnas. When he learned the final bull of excommunication, releasing Philip's subjects from their allegiance to the crown, was to be formally promulgated on September 8 on the doors of the Anagni cathedral, he and Sciarra Colonna with a troop of 600 horse and 1,000 footsoldiers entered the city of Anagni at dawn, and after a long battle in the streets finally broke into the papal palace and confronted the pope, who met them cross in hand, arrayed in his pontifical robes. When he refused to resign, Colonna wanted to kill the aged pontiff, but Nogaret, who as a lawyer opted for some kind of legal trial held under French auspices, intervened.[32] For two days he and Colonna argued as to their next move, while mercenaries looted the palace. But on the third day the populace, recovered from their initial shock, staged a counter-revolution that drove the intruders from the city. Boniface was taken to Rome, but the sick and broken octogenarian never recovered from the assault. On October 11, after making his confession in the presence of eight cardinals, he died quietly.[33]

It was not until the following April that his successor, Pope Benedict XI, lifted the ban on the university and Philip expedited the return of students.[34] If Scotus came back by May he would have begun his lectures with Bk. IV which was scheduled to be read that month.[35] It is in this work that he took up the question of restitution, and in the

---

[32] Nogaret apparently planned to capture the Pope and bring him somehow before an ecclesiastical trial in France. Enough of the French hierarchy were convinced that in view of the seriousness of the charges Boniface ought to call a council to clear himself. Nogaret thought such a council held in French territory could be persuaded to depose him.

[33] Powicke, *art. cit.*, p. 71-72; for an eyewitness account of the attack itself see Master William Hundleby's letter to Bishop Dalderby of Lincoln (edited and translated by H. G. J. Beck, in *art. cit.*, pp. 190-205). If Scotus did spend his exile at Oxford in the Lincoln diocese, he would likely have been informed of these events.

[34] The newly elected pope excommunicated Nogaret, but sought to make peace with Philip. On April 18, 1304, he removed Boniface's ban on the university. About the same time Philip facilitated the return of the students through Picardy (Little, *art. cit.*, p. 577).

[35] Scotus' Paris lectures on Bk. IV contain future references to Bk. II and III (Little, *art. cit.*, p. 579) and Brampton has argued that Bk. IV as contained in the Worcester Cathedral MS F 69 "has the appearance of not belonging to the tradition of Books I, II, and III. It may well be that this Book IV belongs to the second series of lectures" (*art. cit.*, p. 14). If one argues further that inasmuch as the *Ordinatio* was never completely finished and in Bk. IV there are references to a bull of Benedict XI that Scotus saw with his own eyes, it could well be that *Ordinatio* IV may represent a revision done at Paris and not at Oxford as commonly supposed.

aftermath of the political events gave his remarkable analysis of the origin of the state and civil authority that was afterwards incorporated into his *Ordinatio*.[36]

Scotus had plenty of opportunity to reflect on the political claims of the extreme papalists and publicists during the months of his exile. Though he may never have read either Quidort's *De potestate regia et papali*[37] (written between 1302-3) or *De ecclesiastica potestate*[38] of Giles, he must have known of others who held similar views to those of these two key figures in the history of politics. For their opposing theories were discussed in university circles and pamphleteers had popularized them in the streets of the French capital. Furthermore, since John of Paris was a famous Dominican preacher and polemicist, Scotus may well have heard Quidort himself speak on the subject.[39] And the extreme papalist

---

[36] The parallel passages to our present question are in the form of a combined corpus to three questions (*Rep. par.* IV, dist. 15, qq. 2-4). In it he is still concerned with the need to determine at the outset "What is the source of distinct ownership and when did it initially come to be distinguished in such a way that 'this' is called mine and 'that' is called yours, and whence came this distinction?" One of the other questions concerns the obligation to restore the good name of one who has been defamed. Did Scotus bring this up because Philip was still trying to justify the actions of his ministers by bringing Boniface posthumously to trial?

[37] References to John (Quidort) of Paris are from the critical edition of Dom Jean Leclercq, O.S.B. in his study, *Jean de Paris et l'ecclésiologie du XIIIᵉ siècle* (Paris: J. Vrin, 1942), pp. 173-260; and from the English translation J. A. Watt, *John of Paris: On Regal and Papal Power* (Toronto: The Pontifical Institute of Mediaeval Studies, 1971); hereafter referred to respectively as Leclercq and Watt.

[38] References to Giles are from the critical edition of Scholz, *Aegidius Romanus, De ecclesiastica potestate* (Weimar, Herm. Böhlen, 1929, repr. 1961, Scientia Aalen), and the English translation by R. W. Dyson, *Giles of Rome On Ecclesiastical Power*, Dover, NH: Boydell Press, 1986; hereafter referred to as Scholz and Dyson respectively. Like Watt's translation of Quidort, Dyson gives a detailed account of the conflict between Philip and Boniface in his introduction.

[39] As Quidort explained in the *proemium* to his work *On Regal and Papal Power* he sought to strike a middle course between two errors, that of the Waldensians who denied the pope and ecclesiastical hierarchy had any power in temporal affairs or any right to temporal wealth and "the position of Herod who on learning of the birth of a king called Christ believed that his kingdom was of the human kind. Certain moderns seem to have taken their views from this source. For they . . . assert that the pope, in so far as he stands in Christ's place on earth has a power over the property of princes and barons as well as cognizance and jurisdiction of them. They say that the pope has power in temporalities in a more excellent way than the prince because he has primary authority, derived directly from God, whereas the prince has his power mediately from God through the pope. They go on to argue that the pope only exercises this power in certain determinate cases, as the decretal *Per venerabilem* states. It is the prince who has the immediate executive power. . . . If the pope sometimes says he has no temporal jurisdiction, this must be understood as

position Quidort refers to as "opinio quorumdam modernorum." would not have been wholly unknown to him, even if Scotus did not have available the work of Giles whom historians usually regard as its chief representative.[40]

But Scotus was certainly acquainted with some of Giles' earlier philosophical views, perhaps even those of the *De regimine principum* that Giles had written some twenty years before as young prince Philip's tutor.[41] In it Giles not only stressed Aristotle's principle that the State is a natural institution, but in contrast to Aristotle he asserted as a principle that the monarch should be above the law.[42] Scotus by contrast

---

referring to the regular and immediate exercise of jurisdiction, or because he wants to maintain peace between church and princes or to ensure that prelates are not overprone to become occupied with temporal matters and secular business. They argue that the relationship of the pope to temporalities is different in kind from that of princes and prelates. For he is sole true lord in that he can absolve a usurer from the debt he owes through his crime, take from another what otherwise belongs to him and that should he do such an act it is valid, even though he commits a sin in doing it, though he should only do it for the reasonable defense of the church or the like. Other prelates and princes, by contrast, are not lords but guardians, agents, stewards." *Proemium* (Watt, pp. 71-72; Leclercq, p. 174.)

[40] Only Henry of Cremona is cited explicitly by Quidort; the other pro-papalist arguments he attacks are simply referred to as those "I have heard and have been able to collect." (Watt, p. 141; Leclercq, p. 207. Political historians usually point out that James of Viterbo and Augustinus Triumphus held similar views.

[41] Confer the excellent analysis of Giles' earlier work in R. W. Carlyle and A. J. Carlyle, *A History of Mediaeval Political Theory in the West*, vol. V "The Political Theory of the Thirteenth Century" (New York: Barnes and Noble, 1928, p. 13, 75-76). Carlyle sees Giles later work as opposed to this earlier work, but not all historians agree. Did Giles simply keep quiet in the first as to what the status of a national state might be under a Christian dispensation or did he only gradually develop his mature conceptions of the plenitude of power possessed by a pope as the Vicar of Christ? See C. H. McIlwain's discussion of this question (*The Growth of Political Thought in the West*, [New York: Macmillan, 1932], pp. 257-58.

[42] As Carlyle points out: "Aristotle had maintained that the true prince was an instrument of the law, and that it was better to be governed by a good law than by a good king. Egidius states Aristotle's argument as he understood it . . . but only in order to maintain the opposite. While the king is under the natural law, he is not under the positive law. This is indeed a highly significant development of political theory, for this is a thoroughgoing contradiction of the principle of Bracton [*Ipse autem rex non debet esse sub homine sed sub Deo et sub lege*], and practially of all mediaeval theory; for the principle that the king is the servant and not the master of the law belongs not only to the feudal system, but to the whole structure of mediaeval society, and is expressed by practically all the mediaeval writers, except some of the Bologna Civilians. It is, indeed, with Egidius Colonna, as we have said, that we come on the beginning of that conception of the monarchy which was to be developed in the sixteenth and seventeenth centuries." (*Ibid.*, pp. 75-76). We find echoes of this same principle in Giles's *De ecclesiastica potestate* (III, c.

regards law as an expression of the will of the community, the same will that is the immediate source of the ruler's political authority. Far from a ruler being above the law, then, he is bound to legislate in accord with the best interests of the community for the very laws he passes are themselves to be regarded as the will of the community.[43]

Both Giles and Quidort stress that monarchy is the best form of government.[44] Based on the behavior of the rulers he was familiar with, the Scot may have been more skeptical on that subject. At any rate he only insists that whatever form political authority may take, it is the people or the ruler's subjects who give that form of government its authority.

Scotus had no reason to spell out his views on Church/State relationships which were the primary concern of Quidort and Giles. His social contract theory of the origin of political authority, however, is an implicit rejection of Giles' contention that it, like property rights, must be mediated through the papacy.[45] And his third conclusion that such

---

8) where the monarchy becomes the papacy, for there Giles insists that since in the last analysis the pope has no superior under God, he is also above any positive law. "For though the Supreme Priest is a creature without halter and bridle and is a man above positive laws, he ought nonetheless to impose halter and bridle upon himself, and live according to the established laws: and, unless special cases emerge and certain causes require otherwise, he should observe the established laws" (Dyson, p. 187; Scholz, p. 190). Quidort notes that, as papalists interpret this principle, it applies not only to political authority but also to property rights. And historians have been quick to point out that, Giles' argument is not unlike that used in the sixteenth century to support the divine succession of the monarch. As George H. Sabine puts it: "The divine right of a king is a replica, *mutatis mutandis*, of the divine right of the pope" (*op. cit.*, p. 277; see also Carlyle, V, *op. cit.*, p. 76).

[43] In explaining his first conclusion as to how ownership is transferred Scotus writes: "I assume the consent of everyone to be included in the making of the community. Hence, the community has this consent offered already, as it were; and inasmuch as each person consents to the just laws passed by the community or the ruler, the community can transfer the ownership to anyone by means of a just law" (*infra*, p. 47).

[44] Quidort writes: "Government of a community is more effective when conducted by one man, according to virtue, than when exercised by many or few virtuous men." (op. cit., ch. 1; Watt, p. 78; Leclercq, p. 176; for Giles view see Carlyle, *op. cit.*, pp. 75-76.)

[45] As Tierney notes: "The work of Giles of Rome has been much admired by historians of political philosophy for its formidable combination of complexity of thought with coherence of argument. Equally striking, however, was its total failure to convince the contemporary critics of the papacy against whom it was directed. No king ever acknowledged that all temporal power was held from the pope; no representative assembly of towns and nobles ever accepted such a view; no hierarchy of bishops in any country urged it on their ruler; no synod of clergy endorsed it. The idea of a superiority inherent in the papacy because of its total commitment to spiritual values had become too far

property rights were not given by divine law is an implicit repudiation of the claims of Giles of Rome[46] as well as that of James of Viterbo.[47] Indeed, it is almost as if he had these two Augustinian friars in mind, that he quotes St. Augustine to prove his own point of view. Had Scotus been asked about Boniface's own controversial statement to the envoys of King Albert of Hapsburg, "As the moon has nothing that it has not received from the sun, so neither does any earthly power have anything, unless it has received it from ecclesiastical power...all power is from Christ and from us as the Vicar of Christ," the Subtle Doctor might have replied that remark was made to the German king's official ambassadors as papal arbiter of his disputed claim to the Emperor's throne; furthermore it was made on April 30 in response to King's Philip's March request that Christian princes join him and the French clergy in their efforts to have Boniface deposed. Undoubtedly he would

----

removed from the reality of the bureaucratic, worldly minded Roman curia to carry any conviction. Giles of Rome had described a platonic vision that was becoming ever more remote from the real worlds of affairs" (*op. cit.*, p. 195). And P. W. Nash declares "Relying on the analogy of the soul's supremacy over the body, he saw in papal theocracy fulfillment of the Augustinian ideal of the city of God. Although he championed the theory of the 'two swords,' his own fanaticism and pedantry helped to eliminate an outdated papal theocracy" ("Giles of Rome," *New Catholic Encyclopedia*, vol. 6, 485).

[46] What Giles' did in *De ecclesiastica potestate* was to develop not only a new theory of government at odds with the more common populist theory, a version of which Scotus defends, but a new theory of property or material possessions itself. As he puts it most clearly in Bk. II, ch. 7: "We wish . . . to show that there may be no lordship with justice over temporal things or lay persons or anything else which is not under the Church and through the Church: for example, this man or that cannot with justice possess a farm or a vineyard or anything else which he has unless he holds it under the Church and through the Church" (Dyson, p. 68; cf. Scholz, p. 73). And in the following chapter he explains: "You see clearly, then, that kings are worthy possessors of their kingdoms, princes of their principalities, and other faithful people of their possessions, rather through their mother the Church, by whom they are spiritually regenerated, than through their fathers and by paternal inheritance . . . But if a prince, or any one of the faithful says that he receives whatever inheritance he has - be it a principality or any other inheritance - from his father, by whom he was carnally begotten, he ought rather to say that he receives that principality and inheritance from the Church, though whom he is spiritually regenerated and sacramentally absolved. For, by this regeneration and absolution, he who formerly was unworthy begins to be worthy of his inheritance and possession, and he who was once justly liable to be deprived then begins justly to possess" (Dyson, p. 74; Scholz, p. 79).

[47] They both see in the papacy a realization of the ideal Augustine envisioned in Bk. II of the *City of God*. As Giles expresses it: "After the passion of Christ, no commonwealth can be truly such in which Holy Mother Church is not cherished and of which Christ is not the founder and ruler" (Dyson, p. 68; Scholz, p. 73).

have heartily agreed with Pope Pius XII's assessment that "this medieval conception was conditioned by the times."[48]

And while he would have been more sympathetic to Quidort than to Giles's ideas as to how rulers acquire political authority,[49] he differs from Quidort as to the natural law origin of the state.[50] Political

---

[48] *Acta Apostotlica Sedis*, vol. 22 (1955), p. 678. The Pope is explaining how it was that "Quand Notre Prédécesseur Boniface VIII disait, le 30 April 1303, aux envoyés du roi germanique Albert de Habsbourg: '. . . sicut luna nullum aliquid habet, nisi quod recepit a sole, sic nec aliqua terrena potestas aliquid habet, nisi quod recipit ab ecclesiastica potestate . . . omnes potestates . . . sunt a Christo et a nobis tamquam a vicario Iesu Christi'—, il s'agit bien là de la formulation peut-être la plus accentuée de l'idée dite médiévale des relations du pouvoir spirituel et du povoir temporel; de cette l'idée, des hommes comme Boniface tirèrent les conséquences logiques. Mais, même pour eux, il ne s'agit ici normalement que de la transmission de l'autorité comme telle, non de la désignation de son détenteur, ainsi que Boniface lui-même l'avait déclaré au Consistoire du 24 juin 1302. Cette conception médiévale était conditionnée par l'epoque. Ceux qui connaissent ses sources, admettront probablement qui'il serait sans doubt encore plus étonnant qu'elle ne fut pas apparue."

[49] Scotus would undoubtedly agree with Quidort (ch. 10) when he writes: "Royal power existed in its own right in both principle and practice before papal power and there were kings before there were any Christians in France. Therefore in neither principle nor practice does royal power come from the pope but from God and the people who choose a king either as an individual or as a member of a dynasty, as was in fact done formerly. To say that royal power came first directly from God and afterwards from the pope is quite ludicrous" (Watt, 124; Leclercq, p. 199). While Scotus never declared expressly that monarchy was the best form of government, with his familiarity of the English parliamentary system he would undoubtedly agree with Quidort's qualification that it would be better if it were combined with aristocracy and democracy. For Quidort in ch. 19 admits "Although a constitution in which one single individual rules according to virtue is better than any other form of single rule, as the Philosopher shows in Book 3 of his *Politics*, nonetheless, joined with aristocracy and democracy, it is better than the pure form, because, in a mixed constitution, all have some share in government" (Watt, p. 206; Leclercq, p 236). Though Quidort considers monarchy the best form of government, unlike Dante, he does not think there should be a single supreme monarch for the human race as a whole. "We may conclude therefore that the temporal rulership of the world does not demand the rule of a single man as does spiritual rulership, nor can such be deduced from either natural or divine law" (ch. 3; Watt, pp. 85, 87; Leclercq, pp. 180, 181).

[50] Scotus agrees with Augustine in distinguishing carefully between society and the state. The human race is indeed social by nature but its natural grouping is in families that were created to live together in peace and harmony according to the divine law. But in their original condition adults are not bound to obey one another, for, apart from paternal authority, no one has any right of dominion over another person. Scotus also believes with Augustine that the civil power of government is a consequence of sin and a remedy for its evil effects, for it was sin which rendered impossible the continuance of the state of peaceful cooperation between families. He differs from Augustine, however, in that he does not derive the power of princes directly from God like Giles, James of Viterbo, or

authority became necessary only because of man's condition after the fall, a condition not unlike that which Hobbes or Locke envisioned where "those stronger and more belligerent would have deprived others of necessities. Therefore the commonwealth that Aristotle describes in Bk. II of the *Politics*, where all things were not held in common, was much better than that of Socrates, which Aristotle rejected because of the condition in which he found man." Scotus never suggests that any king has a right to determine his successors unless this were expressly given to him by the community.[51] He also places greater stress on the idea that the consent of the whole community is implicit in their acceptance of the just laws promulgated by the ruler or legislative body chosen by the community.[52]

Today, when for the first time in history we can see how our earth looks to the eye of an astronaut, we are in a better position to realize the truth and appreciate the significance of Scotus' basis assumption that "the Lord's is the earth and the fulness thereof." By the law of nature our earthly space ship with its limited resources belongs to the human race as a whole. Scotus as a follower of Francis of Assisi, patron saint of environmentalists, reminds us that no individual has any divine or inalienable right to property that is not mediated through the community. In the Declaration of Independence our founding fathers did well to substitute "the pursuit of happiness" for "property" in John Locke's triad of our inalienable rights.

The other topic that needs to be put in historical perspective is that of usury and/or interest. Both of these interrelated terms at the time of Scotus meant something quite different from what they mean today. Interest, in Roman law, was a lender's title to compensation for the loss suffered because a borrower failed to return the loan on time. It was essentially a damage claim,[53] and never payment for the use of the

---

Quidort, but rather from the consent of the community given in the voluntary compact of the social contract. For where Scotus quotes the decretals of Gratian that "by the law of nature all things are common to all," Quidort in the opening chapter of his work argues that by both the law of nature and that of nations, man is a political and social animal (Watt, pp. 76-79; Leclercq, pp. 176-78).

[51] Like Bellarmine and Suarez, Scotus would have had no sympathy with the theory of the "divine right" of kings, and it would be interesting to discover how far his populist account may have influenced these late scholastics.

[52] See *supra* note 43.

[53] The Latin term *interesse* is a noun derived from the infinitive verb form (*inter esse*) to express the compensation due to an injured party estimated on the basis of the

money.[54] It retained this meaning until the 15th century, when the notion was extended gradually to legitimize a surcharge for any loss the lender might have to bear for making the loan due to change in the fair price of market commodities. Eventually it came to have its present meaning of a charge or price for loanable funds. But interest in this modern sense was practically equivalent to what usury meant at the time of Scotus, whereas usury today refers exclusively to an exorbitant charge of interest.

We live in a commercial age where credit may be called the lifeblood of the economy. It may be difficult to understand why usury in its original sense, or interest in its contemporary meaning, defined as the price for loanable funds, was once condemned by both philosophers and churchmen alike. Plato, Aristotle, Cicero, and Seneca denounced it as inimical to the state. Scholastic philosophers saw it as a violation of commutative justice. Seeing how the greed of the money lenders' could result in exploitation and oppression of the poor, driving them to despair, slavery, and even suicide, both Church and State attempted, often futilely, to regulate it. Medieval preachers like Bernardine of Siena, railed against it as the great vice which corrupted cities and Church alike and held men of property in bondage. To combat the insatiable rapacity of usurers, the taking of interest was strictly forbidden by the third Council of the Lateran (1179), the second Council of Lyons (1274) and shortly after Scotus' death by the Council of Vienne (1311), the last declaring that anyone who maintained that the practice of usury is not sinful should be punished as a heretic.

Scholastics like Aquinas, Bonaventure, or Scotus, considered any charge for the loan of money itself as usury and hence as intrinsically evil. To understand why we must keep in mind the basis for their conception of the nature of a fungible loan in general and of money in particular. A fungible is a perishable or generic good, like coal, lumber, or food, and the loan of such is called a *mutuum*. The loan of a non-fungible good, by contrast, is called a *locatio et conductio*, that is, a contract of leasing and hiring.

"difference between" (quod inter est) his present state and what it would have been had his debtor lived up to his obligation. Only incidentally did it come to be attached to a damage claim on a money loan. Latin jurists never used it in the sense of payment for the use of money.

[54] Jurists employed the Latin term *usura* (= use) to designate payment for the use of money, or to express the monetary increase on the capital investment.

In leasing or hiring, the article loaned, like a boat, a house, or a donkey, is not immediately destroyed or consumed in being used, and hence one can distinguish clearly between the temporary transfer of use and the retention of ownership. In the case of a *mutuum*, however, the individual article is consumed in being used, and hence its ownership as well as its use is transferred.[55] Since the lender no longer owns the article, he has no claim to any profit the borrower can make with what now belongs to him. Commutative justice only requires that what is returned be of the same quantity and quality as what was given. It is unjust, therefore, to demand in addition to the return of the good or its equivalent, an additional charge for its use. In the case of leasing or lending, however, since only the use and not the ownership is transferred, it is the identical article that is returned, and in justice one may charge for the depreciation or other loss to the lender entailed by the use.

Some scholastics argued that where the use of an article involves its consumption, use and ownership cannot be distinguished. As Aquinas puts it: "In those things whose use is their consumption, the use is not other than the thing itself; whence to whomever is conceded the use of such things, is conceded the ownership of those things and conversely."[56] In Scotus' day Richard of Mediavilla, like St. Thomas, made this his principal argument. Scotus reminds Richard, that as a Franciscan he cannot identify use and ownership even in the case of fungibles, for in explaining the Franciscan rule of no private ownership either as an individual or as a community Pope Nicholas III makes clear that a friar is conceded only the use, not the ownership of the necessities of life. This interpretation of Nicholas, Scotus adds, has since been incorporated by Pope Boniface VIII into the corpus of canon law. One must find another reason, then, to show ownership is transferred in the case of a money loan. Scotus finds it in etymological argument used in

---

[55] We find an early expression of this idea in the *Speculum conscientiae*, one of the dubious works attributed to Bonaventure: "There are certain goods, whose use is their consumption, and whose ownership is transferred to the one receiving them, for example, money, grain, and wine, hence one who sells the use of such things is called a usurer, and contracts a sin that is deadly, insofar as it is against a mortal precept of justice, for he sells to another what is not his own, since the ownership has now passed." (c. 2, n. 14; St. Bonaventure, *Opera omnia*, VIII, 633). Aquinas (*De malo*, q. 13, art. 4 corp.) develops this as his principal argument.

[56] St. Thomas Aquinas, *De malo*, q. 13, art. 4, corpus.

Roman law, namely, the very word *mutuum*, means "mine (*meum*) becomes yours (*tuum*)." However, he apparently did not feel entirely comfortable with this argument. For if use is separable from ownership, one could conceivably argue that it is only the use, not the temporary ownership one acquires in borrowing money. This seems to be the import of his remark "Let us grant that the money is still his but still admit that money has no fruit of its nature as some other growing things have."

Aristotle's notion of the sterility of money,[57] however, provided Scotus, as it did other scholastics, with an explanation why usury was condemned by philosophers and theologians alike. Money is by its nature essentially a medium of exchange. As such, it was classed as a fungible, for it was consumed, as it were, in the process of exchange for other goods. The money loan became the most common form of a *mutuum*, and Scotus uses it exclusively in this sense. *Usura*[58] or usury, which originally meant a charge for the use of any fungible, came to mean interest in Aristotle's sense (i.e., "the birth of money from money").

When we reflect on Scotus' economic philosophy we see it as an attempt of a theologian with a powerful analytic mind to give a rationale to the notion of a just economy as expressed largely in the canonical legislation of the Church in his day. This is understandable enough since he is primarily concerned with the obligation for restitution in cases of economic injustice.

If we think his social philosophy is simplistic because it is guided by the two conceptions of peace and justice, recall we live in a age where the interests of multinational corporations often determine political policy of the state, where the Dow Jones industrial average is more important to financiers than the service they provide the community or

---

[57] Aristotle: "There are two sorts of wealth-getting, as I have said; one is a part of household management, the other is retail trade: the former is necessary and honorable, while that which consists is exchange is justly censured; for it is unnatural, and a mode by which men gain from one another. The most hated sort, and with the greatest reason, is usury, which makes a gain out of money itself and not from the natural object of it. For money was intended to be used in exchange, but not to increase at interest. And this term interest, which means the birth of money from money, is applied to the breeding of money because the offspring resembles the parent. Wherefore of all modes of getting wealth this is the most unnatural" (*Politics* I, c. 10 (1058a4-b8).

[58] The Latin term *usura*, which means literally use or enjoyment, became the mercantile name for the use of money, and finally for interest charged for such use.

the welfare of the companies whose stock they manipulate, where employees whose livelihood depends on a company they have supported as junior or quasi-partners in a common economic enterprise fear billion-dollar takeovers by stock speculators interested only in breeding more money from money. Surely our notions of what is legitimate and just in the marketplace needs reassessment and our sense long range consequences of the exploitation of our natural resources reevaluated.

Modern man may not recognize the need to adopt Scotus' radical Franciscan commitment to "go through the world as a pilgrim and stranger," but he would do well to recall on occasion that a supreme consideration in political and economic philosophy should be a genuine concern for each individual's liberty and right to share in the economic development of our God-given heritage. For "the Lord's is the earth and the fulness thereof."

TEXT AND TRANSLATION

UTRUM POENITENS TENEATUR RESTITUERE

IS A PENITENT THIEF BOUND TO RESTITUTION

UTRUM POENITENS
TENEATUR RESTITUERE

Secundo quaero utrum quicumque iniuste abstulerit vel detinuerit
rem alienam teneatur illam restituere, ita quod non possit vere
poenitere absque tali restitutione.[1]

[ARGUMENTA PRO ET CONTRA]

[1] Quod non: quia restitutio nihil est poenitentiae; ergo sine ea
potest esse vera poenitentia. Antecedens probatur, quia non contritio
nec confessio, manifestum est. Nec satisfactio, quia illa est redditio
voluntaria alicuius alias indebiti, ex praecedenti quaestione;[2] sed ista
redditio est alias debiti, quia si homo non pecasset, et haberet rem
alienam, teneretur eam restitutere; ergo etc. Item, posset hoc probari
per partes satisfactionis sub quarum nulla continetur restitutio.

Item, nullus tenetur ad impossibile, quia *qui dicit Deum praecepisse
impossibile*, anathema sit, ut dicit Hieronymus;[3] sed quandoque est
impossibile alienum restituere illi cuius est, ut quando nescitur cuius sit.
Quod potest contingere, sive quia nescit de illo a quo habuit, ubi sit nec
de aliquo sibi propinquo, cui vice eius restituat; sive in aliquo casu, ut si
inveniat alienum, et nesciat cuius sit.

Item, nullus tenetur ad restitutionem sibi magis damnosam, quam
sit res utilis ei cui debet fieri restitutio; sed quandoque, utpote si ille cui
est restitutio facienda agat in remotis, non potest sibi restitui nisi
maiores sumptus ponatur in mittendo sibi quam sit totum quod est
restituendum; ergo in illo casu non tenetur.

AM

9 vera] *om.* M 11 praecedenti] praecedente A 13 eam] illam M 16 ut dicit
Hieronymus] secundum Hieronymum M 16-17 est impossibile] i. e. M 22 sit res] r. s. M
|ei, cui debet sibi] de qua debet fieri M 24 totum] *add.* illud M

[1]*Ordinatio* IV, dist. 15, q. 2 (Codex A 233ra-235va; Codex M 192va-195vb; cf. Vivès
18, 255-357).
[2]*Ordinatio* IV, dist. 15, q. 1 (Vivès 18, 180).
[3]Pelagius, *Libellus fidei ad Innocentiam Papam*, n. 10 (PL 45, 1718), notus *scholasticis ut
Hieronymi explanatio Symboli ad Damasum* (Vide PL 21, 1155; 1161-63).

IS A PENITENT THIEF
BOUND TO RESTITUTION?

I ask: *Is one bound to restitution who may have unjustly taken or retained something belonging to another, so that he could not be truly penitent without making such restitution?*

[ARGUMENTS PRO AND CON]

For the negative:

[ARG. 1] Restitution has nothing to do with penance; therefore without it true penance can exist. The antecedent is proved, for it is clearly not contrition or confession. Neither is it satisfaction, for, according to the preceding question,[1] satisfaction is a voluntary return of something not owed, whereas restitution is the return of something that is now owed [to another]. For, if the man had not sinned and did not have something belonging to another, he would be required to give it back; therefore, etc. Also, one could prove it is not any kind of satisfaction by listing each kind and seeing that restitution falls under none of them.[2]

[ARG. 2] Also, no one is held to the impossible, because according to Jerome,[3] *he who says God commands the impossible, let him be anathema.* But sometimes it is impossible to restore what belongs to another to the person who owns it. This can happen either because one has no idea where the person lives from whom he got it, nor does he know any close relative with whom he might leave it, or—to take another case—suppose he found someone else's property and knows not whose it is.

[ARG. 3] Also, no one is held to restitution where this would involve more damage than it would be useful for the owner to have the article back. At times, however, if that person to whom the restitution has to be made has moved to a distant place, the article cannot be restored to him without it taking more to send it to him than the whole thing to be restored is worth; then in this case one is not bound.

Item, I *Ethicorum*:[1] bonum commune divinius est et praeferendum bono particulari; sed possibile est restitutionem faciendam Petro esse damnosam Paulo restituenti, et in hoc magis damnosam reipublicae, quia scilicet Paulus est magis necessarius reipublicae quam Petrus; ergo in isto casu non tenetur restituere.

[2] Item, quilibet tenetur magis diligere se quam proximum, secundum illud Cantic. 2:[2] *Ordinavit in me charitatem*; ergo quando restitutio est sibi ipsi damnosa, ut si est in extrema necessitate, tenetur magis illud retinere quam ex dilectione alterius alii restituere.

Item, restitutio est facienda in favorem alicuius cui fit; ergo non est facienda quando cedit in damnum eius, nec etiam quando cederet in damnum reipublicae; sed gladius redditus furioso esset ei cui restituitur, in damnum, quia male uteretur eo, et etiam in damnum reipublicae, quia laederet pacem civitatis; ergo etc. Et consimiliter potest argui in casibus, quandocumque restitutio habet vel damnum annexum illi cui fit, vel damnum reipublicae annexum.

Item, adultera concipiente filium ex adulterio, filius putativus mariti defraudat verum heredem hereditate, et tamen non tenetur mulier sibi hereditatem restituere; ergo etc. Minor probatur, quia non posset illud sine sui diffamatione, ad quam nullus tenetur; immo ad eius oppositum, et sequeretur magis malum, scilicet uxoricidium, si martir sciret crimen.

Contra:

Augustinus in *Epistola ad Macedonium*,[3] et ponitur in littera:[4] "Quamdiu res, propter quam peccatum est, non redditur, si reddi potest, non agitur poenitentia, sed fingitur. Et 14, quaestione 4,[5] Non

---

AM

1 *Ethicorum*] add. dicitur quod M 3 damnosam] *add.* reipublicae M 4 magis necessarius] n. m. M 9 illud] *add.* sibi M 10 est facienda] f. e. M 13 etiam] *om.* M 14 potest argui] a. p. M 15 quandocumque] quando M 18 hereditate] *om.* M 21 scilicet] *om.* M

[1] Aristoteles, *Ethica Nicomachea* I, c. 2, (1094b 5-10).
[2] Canticum Canticorum, 2:4: *Ordinavit in me charitatem*.
[3] Augustinus, *Epist.* 153 (ad Macedonium), c. 6, n. 20 (PL 33, 662).
[4] *Magistri Petri Lombardi Sententiae in IV libris distinctae*, lib. IV, dist. 15, c. 7; tom. II (Grottaferrata [Romae]: Collegii S. Bonaventurae, 1981), p. 336.
[5] *Decretum Gratiani*, Secunda pars, causa 14, q. 6, c. 1; *Corpus Iuris Canonici* (Ed. A. Friedberg, Leipzig: Bernhard Tauchnitz, 1879) vol. I, col. 742.

[ARG. 4] Also, according to Bk. I of the *Ethics* it is said that the common good is more divine and is to be preferred to a particular good. But it is possible that restitution made to Peter would be damaging to Paul who is restoring it, and in this regard it would be more damaging to the state, namely because Paul is more necessary to the country than Peter is; therefore in this case one is not bound to restitution.

[ARG. 5] Also, everyone is bound to love self more than neighbor, according to that text of Canticle of Canticles, ch. 2: "He has ordered the charity that is in me"; therefore, when restitution is damaging to oneself, as it is in a case of dire necessity, then one has a greater obligation to keep what belongs to another than he has an obligation in charity to give it back.

[ARG. 6] Also, restitution must be made in favor of him to whom it belongs; therefore it is not to be made when it results in damage to him, nor also when it results in damage to the state; the restitution of a sword to one who is furious, however, would be damaging to him to whom it was restored, because he would use it badly and do damage to the state, for he would destroy the peace of the city; therefore etc. And one could argue that the same would hold good whenever restitution would entail damage either to the one to whom restitution is due or to the state.

[ARG. 7] Also, consider an adulteress who conceives a son as the result of her adultery. The putative son of the husband defrauds the true heir of his inheritance. Nevertheless the woman is not bound to restore this inheritance; therefore etc. Proof of the minor: she could not do so without defaming herself and to this no one is bound; indeed she is obligated to the opposite. And if the husband knew of the crime, a greater evil would follow, namely uxoricide.

To the contrary:

Augustine in his *Letter to Macedonius*, which is cited in the text [of Lombard]: "As long as anything whose possession involves a sin, is not restored, if it can be restored, penitence is not real, but only feigned." And in the [*Decrees of Gratian*] 14, question 6: "Sin is not taken away, unless what is stolen is restored." Also, Exodus 22 commands that what is taken unjustly be restored, and a punishment is added.

demittitur peccatum, nisi restituatur oblatum. Item, Exodi 22,[1] ubi praecipitur reddi iniuste ablata, et additur poena.

[CORPUS QUESTIONIS]

[3] Hic tria sunt videnda: primo unde dominia sunt distincta, ut hoc
5   dicatur meum et illud tuum et istud est fundamentum omnis iniustitiae in contrectando rem alienam, et per consequens omnis iustitia in restituendo eam; secundo quomodo dominia prima distincta iuste transferuntur; tertio ex hoc patebit quae sit iniusta rerum occupatio alienarum seu alterius damnificatio in re temporali; quarto, quando ad
10   restitutionem talis teneatur.

[ARTICULUS I. ORIGO DOMINIORUM RERUM DISTINCTORUM]

[CONCLUSIO 1: DE STATU INNOCENTIAE] De primo sit haec prima conclusio quod de lege naturae vel divina non sunt dominia rerum distincta pro statu innocentiae; immo tunc erant omnia communia.
15   Probatur per illud *Decreti*,[2] dist. 8, c. 1: "Iure naturae sunt omnibus omnia communia," et ad hoc adducitur Augustinus *Super Ioannem*,[3] c. 2, dicens: "Quo iure defendis villas ecclesiae, divino vel humano? Primum ius in scripturis divinis habemus; humanum in legibus regis. Unde quo quisque possidet quod possidet? nonne iure humano? Nam iure divino
20   'Domini est terra et plenitudo eius.' Pauperes et divites nonne humana voluntate una terra portat? Ergo et iure humano dicitur 'haec domus mea est, haec villa mea, hic servus meus.'" Item, ibidem: "Tolle iura imperatoris, quis audet dicere 'haec villa est mea.'" Et post, ibidem: "Per iura regis possidentur possessiones." Et 12, q. 1, *Dilectissimis*:[4]
25   "Communis usus omnium, quae sunt in hoc mundo, omnibus esse

---

AM

4 unde] *add.* rerum M 5 iniustitiae] iustitiae A 6 consequens] *add.* communis vel A 7-8 quomodo dominia . . . transferuntur] *om.* A I tertio] secundo A 9 quarto] tertio A 9-10 ad restitutionem talis] t. a. r. M 15-16 omnibus omnia communia] omnia c. omnibus M 17 vel] an M 20 eius] *om.* M 21 nonne humana voluntate] *om.* M I ergo et] *om.* M 22 meus] *add.* est M 23 est mea] m. e. M 24 regis] regia M

[1]Exodus 22:1-2.
[2]*Decretum Gratiani*, Prima pars, dist. 8, q. 1, c. 1; *Corpus Iuris Canonici* (Ed. A. Friedberg) vol. I, col. 12.
[3]Augustinus, *In Ioannis Evangelium*, tract. 6, n. 25 (PL 35, 1436-1437).
[4]*Decretum Gratiani*, Prima pars, causa 12, q. 1, c. 2; Corpus Iuris Canonici vol. I, col. 676.

[BODY OF THE QUESTION]

Here there are three [preliminary] points to investigate, [and fourth the question itself; thus the division into four articles]: First what is the source of distinct ownership such that this may be called "mine" and that "yours"? For this is the basis of all injustice through misappropriation of another's property and consequently of all justice in restoring it. Second, how are the original ownerships justly transferred? Third, from this it will be clear what is an unjust appropriation another's property or doing another damage in temporal things. Fourth, when is one who is guilty of such bound to restitution?

[ARTICLE I. THE SOURCE OF DISTINCT PROPERTY RIGHTS]

[CONCLUSION 1: BEFORE THE FALL NO PRIVATE PROPERTY] As for the first question, the first conclusion is this: "In the state of innocence neither divine nor natural law provided for distinct ownership of property; on the contrary everything was common." Proof is found in [Gratian's] *Decrees* [dist. 8, ch. 1]: "By the law of nature all things are common to all," where he cites Augustine's commentary on the Gospel of John: "By what law do you defend the real estate of the Church? Is it divine or human? The first is found in the divine Scriptures, the human we have from the law of kings. Whence do we possess what we possess? Is it not by human law? For by divine law 'the earth and the fullness thereof is the Lord's.' And is not the reason the earth bears both poor and rich the will of man? It is by human law, therefore, that we say: 'This house is mine, this farm is mine, this servant is mine." Again in the same place Augustine says: "Remove the Emperor's laws and who will dare say: 'This is my farm'?" And later, in the same work, he adds: "By the king's laws we own our possessions." And in [Gratian's *Decrees*] *Causa* 12, q. 1, *Dilectissimis*: "All men ought to have the common use of everything on earth."

The rationale for this is twofold. According to right reason men should have the use of things in such a way as, first, to contribute to a peaceful and decent life, and [second] to provide needed sustenance. But in the state of innocence common use with no distinct ownership would

debuit."

[4] Ratio ad hoc duplex. Prima, quia usus rerum secundum rectam rationem ita debet competere hominibus sicut congruit ad pacificam conversationem et necessariam sustentationem. In statu autem innocentiae communis usus sine distinctione dominiorum ad utrumque istorum plus valuit quam distinctio dominiorum, quia tunc nullus occupasset quod fuisset alteri necessarium, nec oporteret illud ab ipso per violentiam extorqueri, sed quilibet hoc quod primo occurrisset, occupasset ad usum necessarium. Sic etiam magis fuisset ibi sufficientia ad sustentationem, quam si alicui praecluderetur usus alicuius per appropriationem illius factam alteri.

[5] [CONCLUSIO 2: Post lapsum dominium privatum licitum est] Secunda conclusio est quod istud praeceptum legis naturae de habendo omnia communia revocatum est post lapsum.

Et rationabiliter, propter eadem duo. Primo, quia communitas omnium rerum esset contra pacificam conversationem, cum malus et cupidus occuparet ultra ea quae essent sibi necessaria. Et hoc etiam inferendo violentiam aliis, qui vellent secum eisdem communibus ad necessitatem uti, sicut legitur de Nemroth,[1] qui "erat robustus venator coram Domino," id est, hominum oppressor. Item, esset contra necessariam sustentationem propter illud, quia fortiores bellatores privarent alios necessariis. Et ideo politia Aristotelis II *Politicae*,[2] quod non sint omnia communia, multo melior est quam politia Socratis, quam reprehendit de omnibus communibus secundum istum statum quem Aristoteles invenit in hominibus.

[6] [CONCLUSIO 3: DOMINIUM PRIVATUM PER LEGEM POSITIVAM] Tertia conclusio est quod revocato isto praecepto legis naturae de habendo omnia communia, et per consequens concessa licentia appropriandi et distinguendi communia, non fiebat actualiter distinctio per legem naturae, nec per divinam.

AM

9 occupasset] necessarium fuisset M | necessarium] *om.* M 9 magis] maior M 14 istud] illud M |hominibus] habente M 16 et] *om.* A 20 qui] quod M 26 Aristoteles] Philosophus M | hominibus] omnibus M 29 est quod] *om.* M

[1]Genesis: 10:8-9.
[2]Aristoteles, *Politica* II, c. 5.

have been more conducive to this than individual ownership, for no one would have taken what another needed, nor would the latter have had to wrest it by force from the other; rather each would have taken what first came to hand as needed for that persons' use. In this way also a greater sufficiency for sustenance would have obtained than if one person's use of a thing were precluded because another had monopolized it.

[CONCLUSION 2: AFTER THE FALL PRIVATE PROPERTY IS LICIT] Our second conclusion is this: "After the Fall of man, this law of nature of holding all things in common was revoked."

This also was reasonable, for the same two reasons. First of all, communality of all property would have militated against the peaceful life. For the evil and covetous person would take more than needed and, to do so, would also use violence against others who wished to use these common goods for their own needs, as we read of Nimrod, the first potentate: "He was a mighty hunter before the Lord!"—that is to say, he was an oppressor of men. Secondly, the original law would also have failed to ensure the necessary sustenance of mankind, for those stronger and more belligerent would have deprived the others of necessities. Therefore, the commonwealth Aristotle describes in Bk. II of the *Politics*, wherein all things were not held in common, was much better than that of Socrates, which Aristotle rejected because of the condition in which he found man to exist.

[CONCLUSION 3: PROPERTY RIGHTS BASED ON POSITIVE LAW] The third conclusion is this: "Once this natural law precept of having all in common was revoked, and thus permission was given to appropriate and divide up what had been common, there was still no actual division imposed either by natural or by divine law."

Not by divine law, as the aforesaid citation from Augustine proves—"By what law?" and so on. Not by a law of nature, in all probability. For nothing indicates that the original law was reversed rather than revoked (and the original determination of the law was that all things be common), unless we take to be natural law the proposition in *The Enactments of Justinian*: "Whatever formerly belonged to no one is conceded by natural reason to the first person obtaining possession of the same." For even though it seems clear that, in all probability, a division must take place once natural reason grasped that goods should

Per divinam non, ut probatur per illud Augustini superius
adductum: "Quo iure," etc. Per legem naturae non, ut videtur esse
probabile, quia non apparet quod illa de terminet ad opposita. Ipsa
autem determinavit in natura humana ad hoc quod est 'omnia esse
communia,' nisi dicatur quod illa propositio *Institutionum*,[1] de rerum
divisione "Ferae bestiae": "Quod nullius est in bonis, conceditur
occupanti," sit de lege naturae. Sed licet statim post apprehensionem
naturalem de hoc quod est res esse dividendas, occurrat illa tamquam
probabilis et manifesta, tamen rationabilius est dicere quod ipsa non sit
de lege naturae, sed positiva. Et ex hoc sequitur quod ex aliqua lege
positiva fiebat prima distinctio dominiorum. Igitur ut ista distinctio sit
iusta, oportet videre quomodo lex positiva talis sit iusta.

[CONCLUSIO 4: LEX POSITIVA REQUIRIT AUCTORITATEM] Sit
ergo conclusio quarta quod lex positiva iusta requirit in legislatore
prudentiam et auctoritatem.

Prudentiam, ut secundum rectam rationem practicam dictet quid
statuendum sit pro communitate; auctoritatem, quia lex dicitur a
ligando, sed non quaecumque sententia prudentis ligat comunitatem,
nec aliquem, si nullius praesideat. Quomodo autem prudentia poterit
haberi ad excogitandas leges iustas satis patet. Quomodo autem
auctoritas iusta quae cum hoc requiritur ad legem iustam?

[7] [CONCLUSIO 5: DE AUCTORITATE POLITICA] Sequitur quinta
conclusio, quod est principatus duplex, vel auctoritas, scilicet paterna et
politica. Politica duplex, scilicet in una persona vel in
communitate.—Prima, scilicet paterna, iusta est, scilicet ex lege naturae,
qua omnes filii tenentur parentibus obedire, nec ista per aliquam legem
positivam, Mosaicam vel evangelicam, est revocata, sed magis
confirmata.—Auctoritas vero politica, quae est supra extraneos, sive in
una persona resideat sive in communitate, potest esse iusta ex communi
consensu et electione ipsius communitatis. Et prima auctoritas respicit

---

AM

4 ad hoc] hic M | omnia] omnino M 6 in bonis] om. M 7 sit de] sicut in M | statim]
quasi M 7-8 apprehensionem naturalem] n. a. M 15 Et] om. M | ex aliqua] a M 11 ista M
16-17 quid statuendum sit pro communitate] quid faciendum pro conveniente M 17-18 a
ligando] alligando M 23 scilicet paterna] p. s. A 26 aliquam legem] l. a. M | positivam] om.
M

[1] *Institutiones*, II, tit. 1, "De divisione rerum," n. 12, in *Codex Juris Civilis*, ed. Krueger
(Berolini: Apud Weidmannos, 1954), vol. I, p. 10.

be divided, it seems more plausible to say this was effected by positive law rather than the law of nature. It would follow from this that the first division of property was brought about by some positive legislation. To see why this division was just therefore, we must consider why such a positive law would be just.

[CONCLUSION 4: POSITIVE LAW REQUIRES AUTHORITY] Hence, we have this fourth conclusion: "What a just positive law requires of its legislator is prudence and authority."

Prudence, that he might dictate what ought to be established for the community according to practical right reason. Authority, because "law" is derived from a verb that means "to bind," and not every judgment of a prudent man binds the community, or binds any person if the man is head of nothing. It is clear enough how prudence could have been operative in figuring out just laws. But what of the just authority required if the law is to be just?

[CONCLUSION 5: ORIGIN OF CIVIL AUTHORITY] A fifth conclusion follows: "Authority or rulership takes two forms, paternal and political. And political authority is twofold, that vested in one person and that vested in a group."—The first, namely, paternal authority, is just by natural law in virtue of which children are bound to obey their parents. Neither was this revoked by any positive Mosaic or Gospel law, but rather it was confirmed.—Political authority, however, which is exercised over those outside [the family], whether it resides in one person or in a community, can be just by common consent and election on the part of the community.

The first [or parental sort of] authority regards natural descendants, even though they do not dwell in the same city, whereas the second has to do with those who live together even though there is no consanguinity or close relationship between them. Thus, if some outsiders banded together to build a city or live in one, seeing that they could not be well governed without some form of authority, they could have amicably agreed to commit their community to one person or to a group, and if to one person, to him alone and to a successor who would be chosen as he was, or to him and his posterity. And both of these forms of political authority are just, because one person can justly submit himself to another or to a community in those things which are

descensum naturalem, quamquam non cohabitantes civiliter. Secunda respicit cohabitantes quantumcumque nulla consanguinitate vel propinquitate sibi coniunctos, utpote si ad civitatem aliquam aedificandam vel inhabitandam concurrerunt extranei aliqui, videntes se non posse bene regi sine aliqua auctoritate, poterant concorditer consentire, ut vel uni personae vel communitati committerent illam communitatem; et uni personae vel pro se tantum—et successor eligeretur sicut ipse—vel pro se et tota sua posterioritate. Et ista auctoritas politica utraque iusta est, quia iuste potest quis se submittere uni personae vel communitati in his quae non sunt contra legem Dei, in quibus melius potest dirigi per illum cui se subicit vel submittit quam per seipsum. Ergo habemus complete quomodo poterat condi lex positiva iusta, quia ab habente prudentiam in se vel in consiliariis suis, et cum hoc habente auctoritatem iustam aliquo modo dictorum modorum in ista conclusione.

[8] [CONCLUSIO 6: DE AUCTORITATE POLITICA] Ex his sequitur sexta conclusio quod prima divisio dominiorum potuit esse iusta a lege positiva iusta sive lata a patre sive a principe iuste principante sive communitate iuste regulante vel regente, et hoc modo probabile est factum fuisse.

Nam vel Noe post diluvium filiis suis terras distinxit, quas singuli occuparent pro se vel pro filiis suis et posteris; vel ipsi de communi concordia diviserunt sicut legitur Genesis 13[1] de Abraham et Loth, quia Abraham dedit electionem ipsi Loth quam partem vellet eligere et ipse reliquam acciperet. Vel lex aliqua promulgata est a patre, vel ab aliquo electo ab eis in principem, vel communitate cui ipsamet communitas commisit istam auctoritatem, quae—inquam—lex fuit vel potuit esse quod res tunc non occupata esset primo occupantis, et tunc postea diviserunt se super faciem orbis et unus occupavit unam plagam et alius aliam.

AM

3 sibi] *om.* M 7 vel pro se tantum] t. v. p. s M 7 et] *om.* M 8 sua] sui A 9 uni personae] personae A 9 communitati] communitate M 10 quibus] quo M 11 vel submittit] *om.* M 14 modo] *om.* M 14 conclusione] communitate M 20 terras distinxit] d. t. M 21 pro filiis suis] filiis M

[1]Genesis: 13:5-12.

not against the law of God and as regards which he can be guided better by the person or persons to whom he has submitted or subjected himself than he could by himself. Hence, we have here all that is required to pass a just law, because it would be promulgated by one who possesses prudence either in himself or in his counselors and enjoys authority in one of the several ways mentioned in this conclusion.

[CONCLUSION 6: THE FIRST DIVISION OF PROPERTY]

From this the sixth conclusion follows: "The first division of ownership could have been just by reason of some just positive law passed by the father or the regent ruling justly or by a community ruling or regulating justly, and this is probably how it was done."

For after the flood, Noah divided the earth among his sons, each of which occupied a portion for himself and did the same for his sons and posterity, or else the latter divided it further by common agreement, as we read in Genesis 13 about Abraham and Lot, for Abraham gave Lot his choice and took what remained for himself. Or a law could have been promulgated by a father or by someone elected as ruler or by a group to whom the community gave this authority. This law, I say, was or could have been that anything unclaimed would go to the first occupant, and then they split up and fanned out over the face of the earth, one occupying this area, another that.

[ARTICLE II. TRANSFER OF PROPERTY TO ANOTHER]

As for the second article, I say that the transfer of property to another can be either [a] by way of ownership —where a thing passes from one owner to another—or [b] by way of simple use, where the ownership is retained, but another is given the right to use the property in question. And justice or injustice in transferring the simple use involves different rules than does a just transfer of ownership. And a transfer of ownership can take place by the public authority or that of a ruler, or by the authority of law, or by private authority of the owner who possesses it immediately.

[ARTICULUS II. DE TRANSLATIONE DOMINII]

[9] De secundo articulo, dico quod translatio rerum potest esse vel quantum ad dominium, ut scilicet res a dominio unius transeat ad dominium alterius, vel quantum ad usum sive ius utendi, manente
5 tamen dominio apud eumdem. Et iustiti vel iniustitia in translatione usus difformes habet regulas iustae translationis dominii. Haec ergo translatio dominii potest fieri vel auctoritate publica seu principis, vel auctoritate legis, vel auctoritate privata ipsius domini immediate possidentis.

10 ## [A.—TRANSLATIO DOMINII AUCTORITATE PUBLICA]

[CONCLUSIO 1] De prima translatione sit haec prima conclusio in hoc articulo quod translatio dominii auctoritate legis iustae iusta est. Probatur, quia si lex iusta potuit iuste determinare prima dominia, et non minor est auctoritas legis vel principis quod habeo hic pro eodem
15 post divisionem dominorum quam ante, ergo propter causam eandem et eundem effectum potest iuste transferri dominium postquam fuerat alicui appropriatum.

Et ex hoc dico quod praescriptio in immobilibus et usucapio in mobilibus est iusta translatio. Probatur auctoritate, *Extra de*
20 *Praescriptionibus, Vigilanti*[1] et glossa super illud *aliena*.[2] Probatur etiam per rationem dupliciter, primo sic: iuste potest illud a legislatore statui quod est necessarium ad pacificam conversationem subditorum; sed dominium rei neglectae, sicut negligitur in praescriptione et usucapione, transferri in occupantem, necessarium est ad pacificam conversationem
25 civium, quia si non transferretur dominium in istum occupantem, sed remaneret apud priorem, habentem rem pro derelicta post quantumcumque tempus, essent lites immortales; nam quantumcumque tempus ille qui neglexit, vel haeres suus, repeteret eam rem neglectam,

---

AM

5 tamen] *om.* M 11 prima conclusio] c. p. M 12 hoc] isto M 14 est] *om.* M 15 causam eandem] e. c. M 19 iusta] recta vel iusta A 21 a legislatore statui] s. a. l. M 26 habentem rem pro derelicta] *om.* M 28ff tempus . . . quantumcumque] *om.* M 28 suus] *om.* M I eam] illam M

[1]*Decretales Gregorii* IX, lib. II, tit. 26, cap. 5; *Corpus Iuris Canonici*, vol. II (1881), col. 383.
[2]Vide etiam glossam super *Aliena* [Glossa ordinaria a Ioanne Teutonico, revisa a Bartholomea de Brescia circa 1240, continetur in *Corpore Iuris Canonici* (Venetiis, 1605)].

[A. — Transfer of Ownership by Public Authority

[CONCLUSION 1]: The first conclusion in this article has to do with this first transfer. It is this: "The transfer of ownership by authority of a just law is just." Proof: if a just law could have established the initial ownership and the authority of the law or the ruler that I have for the same matter here and now is no less after the division of ownership than it was before, then it follows that for the same reason and the same purpose the ownership can be justly transferred once it had been appropriated by someone.

From this I say that prescription regarding immobile goods and the acquisition of ownership through use as regards mobile goods is a just transfer. Proof by authority: see the [*Decretals*] on *Prescriptions* under the title *Vigilanti*, and the gloss on "*aliena*." Reason also proves this point in two ways: the first in this fashion: It is just for a legislator to establish that which is necessary for the peaceful coexistence of his subjects. But for the peaceful coexistence of citizens it is necessary that the ownership of abandoned property be transferred to the occupant by way of prescription and ownership acquired through use. For if the ownership were not transferred to the occupant, but remained with the first owner no matter how long a time after he had neglected it, there would be endless quarrels. For after some length of time either the person who had abandoned it or his heir would reclaim the deserted property which by this time had been occupied by another person or persons. Such legal bickering would then ensue that it would be impossible for these quarrels [about ownership] to be decided, since sufficient proof would no longer be available. From such perpetual lawsuits fighting and hatred, perhaps, would result between the litigants and thus the whole peace of the state would be disturbed.

The second reason is because the legislator can justly punish by law transgressions that tend to be detrimental to the state. Since this punishment could also be corporal, a fortiori it could be a pecuniary penalty in the form of a fine. By the same token, then, the legislator can punish a transgressor through a fine of this sort, by assigning that in which he is punished to someone who in this matter is a minister of the law. He who neglects his property for such a length of time, however, is

ab alio vel aliis quantocumque tempore occupatam; et essent tales lites, quod impossibile esset eas descindere, quia nec probationem sufficientem habere, et ex talibus litibus perpetuis essent contentiones et forsitan odia inter litigantes, et sic tota pax reipublicae esset perturbata.

Secunda ratio, quia legislator potest iuste per legem punire transgredientem, cuius trangressio vergit in detrimentem reipublicae, et si poena corporali, multo magis poena pecuniaria, et hoc applicando eam fisco; ergo pari ratione potest eum punire poena tali, applicando illud in quo punitur alicui qui in hoc est minister legis; sed negligens rem suam tanto tempore transgreditur, ita quod eius transgressio est in detrimentum reipublicae, quia in impedimentum pacis; ergo iuste potest lex, sicut rem illam neglectam applicare fisco, ita ad pacem maiorem transferre eam in illum qui tanto tempore occupavit, tanquam in ministrum legis. Et ex hoc patet quomodo debet intelligi illa praesumptio iuris et de iure contra quam non admittitur probatio, quia scilicet sic negligens rem suam habuit eam pro derelicta. Etsi enim hoc non sit verum in re, tamen legislator punivit ipsum ac si eam habuisset pro derelicta, quia in aliquo assimilatur habenti pro derelicta, et in illud in quo assimilatur derelinquenti, iuste requirit similem poenam. Istud etiam apparet probabile per hoc quod, si quilibet possit suum dominium transferre in alium, tota communitas posset cuiuslibet de communitate transferre dominium in quemlibet (quia in facto communitatis suppono includi consensum cuiuslibet); ergo illa communitas habens istum consensum quasi iam oblatum per hoc quod quilibet consensit in leges iustas condendas a communitate vel principe, potest per legem iustam cuiuslibet dominium transferre in quemlibet.

[B.—TRANSLATIO DOMINII VEL USUS A PERSONA PRIVATA]

[11] Secundo potest fieri translatio per actum personae privatae immediate habentis dominium re. Hoc autem potest esse vel per actum mere liberalem, vel per actum secundum quid liberalem. Primus est quando transferens nullam expectat redditionem. Secundum est quando pro eo quod transfert, expectat aliquid sibi reddi.

AM

12 pacem maiorem] m. p. M | eam] *om.* M | illum] aliquo M 15 quia] quod M 15 quia] quod M 24 per hoc] in hoc M 26 transferre] transferri M 29 per actum] *om.* M

a transgressor, such that his transgression is to the detriment of the state, because it is a hindrance to peace. Hence a law can be just that assigns as a fine the neglected property itself, so that for the sake of greater peace the property is transferred to the person, as minister of the law, who has occupied it for such a period of time. From this it is clear how one should understand that presumption of law and the law itself against which no proof is admitted, namely that which regards things that have been neglected in this way as having been abandoned. For even though this is not true in reality, nevertheless the legislator punishes this neglect as if the property had been abandoned. For in some respect it does resemble abandoned property, and to that extent it justly requires a similar punishment. Another reason this appears to be probable is that if an individual could transfer his ownership to another, then the community as a whole could transfer the ownership of anything pertaining to the community to anyone. For I assume the consent of everyone to be included in the making of the community. Hence, the community has this consent offered already, as it were; and inasmuch as each person consents to the just laws passed by the community or the ruler, the community can transfer the ownership to anyone by means of a just law.

[B.—TRANSFER OF OWNERSHIP OR USE BY A PRIVATE PERSON]

Secondly the transfer [of ownership] can occur or take place through the act of a private person having ownership of the thing in question. But this can be either through a purely free act or through an act that is free in a qualified sense. The first is when the person making the transfer expects no recompense. The second is when the party making the transfer expects something in return.

[I.—TRANSFER BY A PURELY GRATUITOUS ACT]

[CONCLUSION 2] As for the first, there is this conclusion, which is the second of this article. "The owner of something who is not prohibited by law or by a superior on whose will he depends as to what he gives or transfers, can give his property to another willing to receive it."

[I.—TRANSLATIO PER ACTUM MERE LIBERALEM]

[Conclusio 2] De primo sit haec conclusio quae est articuli huius secunda: Dominus alicuius rei non probibitus a lege seu superiori, a cuius voluntate dependeat in dando vel transferendo vel donando, potest rem suam donare alii volenti recipere.

Hoc probatur, quia ex quo per actum voluntatis suae fuit dominus, ergo per voluntatem potest cessare esse dominus, et alius vult recipere, ergo potest incipere dominus, et non prohibet aliqua causa superior istum desinere et illum incipere esse dominum; ergo per donationem istam fit vere et iuste translatio dominii.*

Ex hoc patet quid requiritur ad iustam donationem, quia liberalis traditio ex parte donantis, et voluntas recipiendi ex parte illius cui fit donatio, et libertas ex parte amborum, huius donandi et illius recipiendi, et quod nulla lege superiori prohibeatur iste vel ille, nec per actum alterius a quo dependeat in ista translatione. Et propter defectum primi non potest quis donare pecuniam Fratri Minori, quia ille non vult esse dominus. Propter defectum secundi non potest Monachus dare praeter Abbatis licentiam, nec filius familias sine voluntate parentis vel parentum; nec etiam clericus in aliquo casu sine voluntate, vel saltem contra voluntatem, domini Papae, ut habetur *Extra de Censibus, Romana*.[1] Ad cuius capituli observationem poenam posuit Gregorius X, cuius capitulum est hodie in 6 libro *Decretalium*, *Exigit*,[2] scilicet quod visitantes a visitatis nulla recipiant manuscula, et si receperint, duplum teneantur restituere, vel non absolvantur a maledictione, quam ipso facto incurrunt, ut dicitur in 6 libro, in novis constitutionibus.[3]

Huic autem correspondet in translatione usus liberalis accomodatio, et habet similes leges ad hoc quod sit iusta, quia requirit in accomodante liberam voluntatem, et in recipiente quod velit recipere rem accommodatam ad usum, et quod non sit aliqua voluntas legis vel principis obsistens illi accommodationi.

AM

1 articuli huius secunda] s. a. h. M 7-8 et alius . . . incipere dominus] *om.* A 8 aliqua causa superior] superiorem causam M 18-19 vel parentum] *om.* 19 clericus] cancellarii *add.* M 20 domini] *om.* M 26 Huic] Hic M. 28 liberam] *add.* vel liberalem A 29 legis] Regis M

[1]*Sextus Decretalium*, lib. III, tit. 20, c. 1; *Corpus Iuris Canonici*, vol. II, col. 1056.
[2]Ibid., c. 2, col. 1057.
[3]Ibid.

Proof of this: from the fact that someone became the owner through an act of the will, that person can also cease to be the owner through an act of the will. The other party wishes to receive it and can, therefore, begin to be the owner. Now there is no higher legal reason that prohibits the one from ceasing to own or the other from becoming the owner. Through such a donation, then, a transfer of ownership truly and justly takes place.

From this it is clear what is required for a donation to be just, for a free transfer on the part of the donor and the will to receive on the part of the recipient, together with [1] freedom on the part of both, of this one to give and that one to receive, and [2] no prohibition either by a higher law or by a person on whom either party would depend for this transfer. Since the first condition is lacking, one cannot give money to a Friar Minor, since he has no wish to be an owner. Because the second condition is lacking, a monk could not donate without his abbot's permission, nor could a son give familial property without the will of a parent or parents, nor in certain cases also a cleric without the will—or at least against the will—of the Pope, as one gleans from the canon *Romana* under the title *De Censibus*, and Gregory X has added a penalty to ensure its observance. It is found today in *Book Six of the Decretals*, and states that canonical Visitors shall not receive any little gift from those whom they visit, and if they do receive such, they are bound to restore it twofold. Otherwise they may not be absolved from the condemnation they incur ipso facto, as is stated in the new constitutions[4] in *Book Six*.

What corresponds to this in the transfer of the simple use, however, is a free loan, and this has similar laws to ensure that the loan is just. For it requires free will on the part of both the lender and the recipient who wants to receive the things loaned for his use. Furthermore, there must be no intent of the law or will of the ruler opposed to such a loan.

[II.—TRANSFER OF OWNERSHIP OR USE BY CONTRACT]

There is another transfer or loan that is not completely free. It is one where the one making the transfer expects something equivalent to what he transfers, and this is properly called a contract, because here the wills are literally *contracted* (that is "drawn together"). For this person

[II.—TRANSLATIO DOMINII VEL USUS IN CONTRACTU]

[12] Alia[1] est translatio non mere liberalis, sed ubi transferens exspectat aliquid aequivalens ei quod transfert, et dicitur proprie contractus, quia ibi simul trahuntur voluntates partium; trahitur enim iste ad transferendum in illum a commodo quod exspectat ab illo vel quod exspectat transferendum in se.

Huiusmodi contractus in quibus dominia transferuntur, quidam sunt rei utilis pro re utili immediate, sicut vini pro blado, et huiusmodi, et dicitur rerum permutatio do ut des vel do si des. Quidam rei utilis pro numismate, vel e converso, quia enim difficile erat res usuales immediate commutare; ideo inventum est medium per quod talis commutatio faciliter fieret, quod vocatur numisma; et dicitur commutatio numismatis pro re usuali emptio, e converso vero venditio. Quaedam vero numismatis pro numismate, et dicitur mutui datio et mutui acceptio.

Sunt ergo quinque contractus, in quibus transfertur dominium, quibus correspondent aliqui contractus in quibus transfertur usus, vel ius utendi, retento dominio. Nam rerum permutationi correspondet mutua vel permutata accommodatio; emptioni correspondet conductio, et venditioni locatio; mutui acceptationi non correspondet aliquid proprie in translatione usus rei.

[1.—DE RERUM PERMUTATIONE]

[13] [CONCLUSIO 3] De prima translatione, scilicet rerum permutatione, sit haec conclusio, quae est tertia huius articuli: Quod domini rerum iuste eas permutant, si sine fraude servant aequalitatem valoris in commutatis secundum rectam rationem, intelligendo hic condiciones prius expositas ad donationem iustam. Explicantur aliae, quae sunt propriae ad iustam permutationem.

[PRIMA CONDITIO] Quod primo additur *sine fraude*, excludit fraudem in substantia, in qualitate et in quantitate. *In substantia*, ut non commutetur aurichalcum pro auro, nec aqua pro vino. *In quantitate*, ut

AM

1 est] om. M 2 et]om. M 5 a] aliquo M 9 rerum] rei M 13 usuali] utili M 14 quaedam vero] tertio mutatio M 16 quinque] sex M 20 locatio] *add.* mutuationi, id est M 25 servant] servent M 30 et in quantitate] *om.* M 31 quantitate] qualitate M

[1] *Sextus Decretalium*, lib. III, tit. 20, c. 2; *Corpus Iuris Canonici*, vol. II, col. 1057.

agrees or contracts to transfer something to another in return for some advantage that he of she expects to be transferred to themselves.

Some contracts in which ownership is transferred concern the direct exchange of things destined for immediate use, such as wine for grain, and this exchange is called *barter* ("I give that you may give" or "I give, if you give."). In others coins are exchanged for something useful or vice versa. The reason for this is that it was difficult for usable things to be exchanged immediately and therefore a means was devised, called a *coin* or piece of money, whereby such an exchange could take place. This exchange of coins for some usable things is called *buying* and the converse is called *selling*. A third type of exchange, coins for coins, is called *loaning money* or *borrowing money*.

There are five contracts, then, in which the ownership is transferred and to these correspond some contracts in which the use or the right to use is transferred while the ownership is retained. A *mutual accommodation* [i.e., the loan of a fungible good or the temporary use of a non-fungible good][5] corresponds to barter; to *buying* corresponds hiring and to *selling* corresponds leasing. As for accepting a money loan, there is nothing that corresponds properly to a simple transfer of its use.[6]

[1.—DIRECT EXCHANGE OF GOODS]

[CONCLUSION 3] Concerning the first transfer, namely, the exchange of things there is this conclusion, which is the third of this article: "The ownership of things is justly exchanged, if in the things exchanged equality of value according to right reason is observed and there is no fraud involved, keeping in mind here the conditions required for a just donation that were set forth earlier." We explain these other features that are proper to a just exchange.

[FIRST REQUIREMENT] The first of these added requirements is that *the exchange must be without fraud*. This qualification excludes fraud as to substance, quantity and quality. As to "substance," for instance, that copper is not exchanged as gold, nor water as wine. As to "quantity" (whether this be measured by (a) weight or (b) some linear measure such as a yardstick or some similar gauge of length, or (c) some other bulk measure, liquid or dry, such as a gallon, a pint, or the like) so that in the

scilicet sive quantitas mensuretur per pondus sive per aliam mensuram, scilicet virgam vel huiusmodi quantum ad longitudinem, vel mensuram aliam corporalem, ut scilicet sextarium modium vel huiusmodi, sive in liquidis sive in aridis, iustum pondus, et universaliter iusta mensura
5 servetur. Consimiliter *in qualitate*, quod non commutetur vinum corruptum quod accipitur pro alio commutante tanquam vinum purum.

[14] Et haec omnia probantur *Extra de Iniuriis et damno dato, Si culpa*:[1] "Qui occasionem damni dat, damnum dedisse videtur." Sed defraudans in substantia istum qui putat permutando accipere aliam
10 substantiam, vel in quantitate qui putat accipere aliud quantum, vel in qualitate qui putat accipere aliud quale dat occasionem damni, quia ille non permutaret nisi crederet aliam substantiam, quantitatem et qualitatem recipere; ergo videtur non tantum <fallacia> *De libro Elenchorum*,[2] sed praesumptione iuris et secundum veritatem damnum
15 dedisse.

[Secunda conditio] Sequitur in illa regula quod *aequalitas valoris est servanda*, quod probatur per Augustinum XIII *De Trinitate*, cap. 3:[3] "Vili velle emere et care vendere revera vitium est." Et hoc intelligo de re vili et cara quantum ad usum, quia frequenter quae est res in se nobilior in
20 esse naturali, minoris est valoris et minus utilis usui hominum, et per hoc minus pretiosa, secundum Augustinum *De civitate Dei* libro:[4] "Melior est in domo panis quam mus," cum tamen vivum sit nobilius simpliciter non vivo in esse naturae, et propter hoc additur, "secundum rectam rationem," attendentem videlicet naturam rei in comparatione
25 ad usum humanum, propter quem ista commutatio fit.

[15] [ADEST LATITUDO IN AEQUALITE] Ista autem aequalitas secundum rectam rationem non consistit in indivisibili, ut dicit quidam

---

AM
3 sextarium modium] m. s. M 4 pondus] *om.* M 5 commutetur] *add.* in A 9-10 aliam substantiam] s. a. M | vel] *add.* qualitatem vel quantitatem M | in quantitate] *om.* M 10-11 vel in . . . aliud quale] *om.* M 12 substantiam] *add.* et M 12-13 et qualitatem] *om.* M 17 quod probatur] hoc probatur M | XIII De] *om.* M 17 cap.] *om.* A | care] *add.* velle M 18 intelligo] intelligendo M 19 est res] *om.* M | se] *add.* est M 20 et minus utilis] *om.* M 21 Dei libro] libro vel M 22 sit nobilius] n. sit et M 24 videlicet] secundum M 25 ista commutatio] c. i. M

[1]*Decretales Gregorii* IX, lib. V, tit. 36, cap. 9; *Corpus Iuris Canonici*, II, col. 880.
[2]Aristoteles, *De Sophisticis elenchorum*.
[3]Augustinus, *De Trinitate* XIII, c. 3, n. 6 (PL 42, 1017).
[4]Augustinus, *De civitate Dei* IX, c. 16 (PL 41, 331).

exchange of dry or liquid substances a just weight and in general a just measure be observed. The same holds good as regards "quality" so that soured wine or vinegar is not passed off or sold as pure wine.

And all these are proved [canonically] from the [*Decretals of Gregory IX*]: "Whoever provides the occasion for harm, appears already to have done the harm." But that person provides the occasion for harm to one who thinks in the transaction he is getting another substance, or another amount or another quality of goods. For the person swindled would not have made the exchange unless he believed he was receiving some other substance, or amount or quality. Therefore it seems there is not just an error of judgment (such as we find in discussed in [Aristotle's] *Sophistical Refutations*), but true harm has been done and the law presumes such.

[SECOND REQUIREMENT] What follows in that rule is that *equality of value must be observed*. This is proved from Augustine's *De Trinitate* XIII, ch. 3: "To want to buy what is vile and sell what is dear is truly a vice." And this must be understood of things that are vile and dear so far as use is concerned, because frequently a thing which in itself is more noble in its natural being is less serviceable for the practical for human use and on this score is less precious, according to what Augustine says in *De civitate Dei* XI, ch. 16: "In the home bread is better than a mouse". Nevertheless, every living thing is more noble by nature than what is not living. And because of this it is added: "according to right reason," namely one must attend to the nature of the thing in relation to human use, which is the reason why this exchange takes place.

[EQUALITY ALLOWS FOR A CERTAIN LATITUDE] This equality according to right reason, however, does not consist in what is indivisible [and hence precise], as a certain doctor [Richard of Mediavilla] maintains, motivated by this that justice alone has a real mean whereas the other virtues have only a conceptual mean. But this is false, as was pointed out in Bk III.[7] Indeed there is great latitude in this mean that commutative justice regards or looks to, and within this latitude one does not attain an indivisible point of equivalence between one thing and another, because so far as this is concerned, it is impossible as it were to bring about an exchange [that is precisely equivalent] and it becomes just in any degree between these extremes.

Doctor,[1] motus ex hoc quia iustitia habet tantum medium rei sed caeterae virtutes tantum medium rationis. Hoc enim est falsum, ut declaratum est libro 3 dist.[2] Immo in isto medio quod iustitia commutativa respicit est magna latitudo, et intra illam latitudinem non
5 attingendo indivisibile punctum aequivalentiae rei et rei, quia quoad hoc esset quasi impossibile commutantes attingere. In quocumque gradu citra extrema fiat, iuste fit.

Quae autem sit ista latitudo et ad quantum se extendat, quandoque ex lege positiva, quandoque ex consuetudine innotescit; lex enim
10 rescindit contractum ubi contrahens decipitur ultra medietatem iusti pretii, tamen infra illud, si ex alio appareat iniustitia, debet restitutio fieri correspondens.

Quandoque autem relinquitur ipsis commutantibus, ut pensata mutua necessitate reputent sibi mutuo dari aequivalens hinc inde et
15 accipere. Durum est enim inter homines esse contractus in quibus contrahentes non intendant aliquid de illa indivisibili iustitia remittere sibi mutuo, ut pro tanto omnem contractum concomitetur aliqua donatio. Et si iste est modus commutantium, quasi fundatus super illud legis naturae: *Hoc facias alii, quod tibi vis fieri,* satis probabile est quod
20 quando sunt mutuo contenti, mutuo volunt sibi remittere si quae deficiunt ab ista iustitia requisita.

[2.—IUSTITIA IN EMPTIONE ET VENDITIONE]

[16] Consimilis conclusio omnino est de iustitia in emptione et venditione, quia ita ibi oportet ex una parte considerare numisma, sicut
25 hic rem mutatam. Addo quod in istis contractibus utriusque *licet permutantem vel vendentem pensare damnum suum, non autem commodum ipsius ementis sive cum quo permutat.* Hoc dico *in carius vendendo vel permutando; et intelligo sic,* si quis multum indiget sua re et per magnam

---

AM

1 motus ex hoc quia] quod M 2 Hoc] Hic M | declaratum est] declaratur M 6 communtanes] commutations vel commutantes A 7 citra] circa A 13 pensata] *om.* M 15 est enim] enim est M 15 quibus] quo M 16 iustitia] *add.* aliquid M 18 est] *om.* M 20 quae] quid M 25 Addo] *add.* vel ad eo A 25 contractibus utriusque] u. c. M 27 Hoc dico] Hic omnino M 28 sua re] r. s. M

[1]Richardus de Mediavilla, *Sent.* III, dist. 33, art. 3, q. 4 (Brixiae, 1591), t. III, p. 389-90.

[2]Deest in *Ordinatione* et opere Parisiensi.

But what this latitude is and to what it extends is known sometimes through positive law, and at other times through custom. For the law rescinds a contract where the one contracting is deceived about an average price that is far above what is just. But if it is so far below what it should be that an injustice is done, restitution must be made.

At times, however, it is left to those making the exchange that, after weighing their mutual needs, they decide as to what equivalent must be given and accepted here and there. For among men it is hard for contracts to exist where the contracting parties do not intend to set aside something of that exact or indivisible justice owed to one another, so that to some extent a donation accompanies every contract. And if this is the manner in which these persons engage in the exchange, based, as it were, upon this law of nature: *Do to another as you would wish done to you*, it is sufficiently probable that when they are mutually satisfied, if there is any deficiency in regard to what justice requires, they mutually intend to waive the difference.

[2.—JUSTICE IN BUYING AND SELLING]

The conclusion is entirely similar as regards just selling and buying, because there it is necessary on the one side to consider the coin as the thing exchanged here. I add, that in both of these contracts *although the trader or vendor thinks he suffers some loss, it is not something advantageous to the buyer or the one with whom he makes the exchange.* I say this in regard to sales or exchanges made at a *price higher than their worth* and I understand it in this way. If someone has great need of his property and yet is induced through the aggressive urging of another to sell or exchange it for something else, since he could compensate himself for the sizable damage he suffers, he can charge more dearly than he would otherwise do if he suffered no such harm. But if the one buying it gains a considerable advantage from what is sold to him, the vendor cannot charge him more dearly. For just because what I own is of greater benefit to him does not make it more precious in itself, or any better to me, and therefore I should not raise the price. But it is otherwise when I am harmed, because then what I own is more precious to me, although it is not so in itself.

instantiam alterius inducatur ab eo ut vendat eam vel permutet pro alia re, cum posset praeservare se indemnem, et ex venditione vel permutatione ista multum damnificatur, potest carius vendere quam si alias sine tali damnificatione venderet vel permutaret. Sed si emens
5 magnum commodum consequitur ex re illa vendita vel permutata, non potest carius vendi vel permutari, quia maius commodum consequitur ex re illa sibi vendita, nam propter maius commodum eius quod consequitur nec res mea est in se pretiosior nec mihi melior, et ideo non debet mihi maius pretium apportare. Secus autem est quando
10 damnificor, quia tunc est mihi pretiosior, licet non in se.

[DE ACCOMMODATIO, CONDUCTIONE ET LOCATIONE] Cum istis contractibus, ut dictum est, conveniunt mutua accommodatio, conductio, et locatio; et consimiliter quantum ad positas iam condiciones est servanda iustitia, considerando ibi ad usum, sicut hic ad
15 dominum.

[3.—DE MUTUI DATIONE]

[17] [CONCLUSIO 4] De ultimo contractu, scilicet de mutui datione, sit haec quarta conclusio istius articuli. De iuste contrahendo, oportet servare aequalitatem simpliciter in numero et pondere, exceptis
20 quibusdam casibus de quibus dicetur in fine.

Ratio huius a quodam[1] assignatur talis, quia usus pecuniae est eius consumptio; ergo concedens eam mutuo, consumit eam.—Contra istud obicitur per illud *"Extra de verborum significationibus: Exiit qui seminat*, et est hodie in *sexto libro*,[2] quod quarumdam rerum usus perpetuo separatur
25 a dominio.

Potest ergo ratio talis assignari, quia in mutui datione transfertur dominium; hoc enim sonat vocabulum, *mutuo do tibi meum*: ergo qui concedit mutuo, non manet dominus pecuniae mutuatae, et per

---

AM

2 cum posset] ut possit M 2 praeservare se] s. p. M 3 ista] illa M 4 sine] cum M 8 consequitur] sequitur M 1 nec res] res M 1est] non est M 18 quarta conclusio] c. quarto M 1 De] Ad M 18 contrahendo] contrahendum mutuum M 21 huius] eius M 23 verborum] *om.* M

[1]Richardus de Mediavilla, *Sent.*, lib. IV, dist. 25, art. 5, q. 5. (Brixiae, 1591), tom IV, p. 223.

[2]Exiit qui seminat (Nicholaus III) in *Sextus Decretalium*, lib. V, tit. 12, cap. 3; *Corpus Iuris Canonici* II, col. 1109.

[LENDING, HIRING AND LEASING] Similar to these contracts [of selling and buying], as was said, are those about lending, hiring, and leasing. And justice demands that the same conditions be observed in regard to the things to be used as are required for ownership.

[3.—CONTRACTS ABOUT LENDING MONEY]

[CONCLUSION 4] The fourth conclusion of this article concerns this last contract about giving a money loan. "To make the contract just, it is necessary to observe without qualification equality as to number and weight except for certain exceptional cases stated at the end."[8]

The rationale given for this by one doctor[9] is that, since the use of money represents its consumption, to give it to another as a loan is to consume it. —An objection to this, however, is the fact that, according to the *Exiit qui seminat*, [of Pope Nicholas III] (incorporated today into *Book Six* of the [*Decretals*] under the title *De verborum significationibus*), the use of certain things is separated forever from their ownership.[10]

Therefore, this sort of reason can be assigned. It is because, in giving a loan, the ownership itself is transferred; for this is what the word *mutuum* (*meum/tuum*) means:[11] "I make mine (*meum*) yours (*tuum*)." Therefore, he who makes the loan does not remain the owner of the money loaned, and as a consequence, if for that money he receives something beyond the principal owed to him, he receives it for something that is not his, or sells what does not belong to him.

Another reason is this; let us grant that the money remains his but still admit that money has no fruit of its nature as some other growing things have. Rather, it only bears fruit because of some one's industry, namely that of the user. But the industry of this user does not belong to the one who loaned the money; hence, to want to receive the fruit of the money is really a desire to have the fruit of another's industry but which the other has not given to him. And that is why, by contrast, the fruit of borrowed things that are fertile is reckoned as part of the principal.

[EXCEPTIONS TO THE RULE] Two cases in general are excepted in this matter of borrowing money. For to receive back more than the capital is licit at times by reason of a contract or pact, at other times it may be licit even without any pact.

consequens, si pro illa pecunia recipit aliquid ultra sortem, pro non suo recipit, sive vendit non suum.

Alia ratio est, esto quod pecunia maneret sua, tamen illa pecunia non habet ex natura sua aliquem fructum, sicut habent aliqua alia ex se germinantia, sed tantum provenit aliquis fructus ex industria alicuius, scilicet utentis.[1] Industria autem huius non est eius qui concedit pecuniam; ergo ille volens recipere fructum de pecunia, vult habere fructum de industria aliena, quam tamen non dedit ille alius sibi, ex hoc quod accepit mutuum ab illo alio. Et haec est ratio quare per oppositum fructus pignorum germinantium computatur in sortem.

[EXCEPTIONES] Excipiuntur in ista mutuatione duo casus in genere: quandoque enim potest aliquis accipere licite ultra capitale ex pacto; quandoque non ex pacto.

[EX PACTO] Primum tripliciter, scilicet: vel ratione poenae conventionalis, dum tamen non fiat in fraudem usurarum; verbi gratia, ego indigeo pecunia mea ad mercandum, concedo tamen tibi ad certum diem adiciens poenam condicionalem quod nisi tali die solvas, quia multum damnificabor alia, solves postea tantum ultra. Haec poena adiecta licita est, quia licet me servare indemnem, sic praemonendo illum cum quo contraho. Signum autem quando non est in fraudem usurarum, manifestum est istud quod quando mercator magis vellet pecuniam sibi solvi die praefixo quam in die crastino cum poena addita vel adiecta. Et per oppositum est in fraudem usurarum quando vult diem transiri potius quam pecuniam in ipso die solvi.

Secundum est ratione interesse. Debitor enim ex cuius non solutione creditor notabiliter damnificatur, tenetur de iustitia satisfacere creditori de interesse. Et licet iste creditor non posset habere contra eum actionem in foro exteriori, utpote quia non sunt pacta forte in ista vel mutuata, tamen in foro conscientiae tenetur debitor ultra sortem ad interesse.

Tertia conditio est quando utrumque, scilicet capitale et illud superfluum, ponitur sub incerto, quod probatur *Extra de Usuris*,

---

AM

8 quam] quod M | alius sibi] s. a. M 9 quare] quasi M 11 aliquis accipere] a. aliquis M 14 scilicet] *om.* M 16 ego indigeo] esto indiges A 19 me] mihi M 21 istud quod] isto M 23 vel adiecta] *om.* M 23 usurarum] *om.* M 28-29 forte . . . mutuata] *om.* M

[1]*Sextus Decretalium*, lib. V, tit. 12, cap. 3; *Corpus Iuris Canonici* II, col. 1109.

[BY REASON OF A PACT OR CONTRACT] Where a pact is concerned, there is a triple way in which a surcharge is licit. First by reason of an agreed upon penalty that is not usurious.[12] For example, I need my money for business, but I give you a certain terminal date for repayment, after which I add a conditional penalty for non-payment on the grounds that I will suffer considerable loss if you delay payment beyond that day. This added charge is licit, since I am allowed to guarantee myself against such a monetary loss, and so forewarn the person with whom I contract. When a merchant would rather be paid by the agreed upon date than exact the additional penalty on the morrow, this is a clear sign that he is not guilty of the fraud of the usurers. On the other hand, he is fraudulent if he wishes the day for payment would pass, rather than receive his money by that date.

The second case is by reason of interest;[13] for the debtor, whose non-payment notably damages his creditor, is obliged in justice to satisfy the creditor by paying interest. And although the creditor has no legal grounds for taking action in the external forum, especially if there is no pact or contract, nevertheless in the forum of conscience the debtor is bound to pay additional interest.

The third condition is where both, namely the capital investment and the surcharge, are subject to uncertainty.[14] This is proved from the title *De Usuris*, chapter *Naviganti*, paragraph *Ratione*[15] using the dialectical argument "From similarity." For if the uncertainty excuses there, it also excuses here.

[WITHOUT A FORMAL AGREEMENT][16] It is also licit without a pact: for only to have the intention or mind alone without any verbal agreement, or other equivalent sign indicating to the debtor that the person making the exchange would not do so without some hope of gain, does not make the recipient of something over and above the capital where there is no pact involved, an unjust possessor of what belongs to the other, and hence there is no obligation to make restitution.

[LOANING MONEY FOR ITS INTRINSIC VALUE] It must also be understood that money has some useful value by very nature, as something to be seen, or as an ornament, or to show one's potential as a wealthy person, and on that score it can be leased, just as a horse or

Naviganti, paragrapho *Ratione*[1] et etiam ratione arguendo per locum a simili,[2] quia sicut ibi incertitudo excusat, ita hic.

[19][SINE PACTO] Sine omni pacto etiam licet, quia solus animus, sine omni pacto verbali vel alio signo aequivalenti ostendente debitori
5 quod mutuans non mutuaret sine spe lucri, non facit istum, accipientem ultra sortem sine pacto, habere alienum, et ideo nec teneri ad restitutionem.

[LOCATIO PECUNIAE] Intelligendum est etiam quod pecunia habet aliquem usum utilem ex propria natura, utpote ad videndum, vel
10 ornandum, vel ostendendum possibilitatem tamquam divitem, et ad istum finem potest locari, sicut equus, vel aliud locabile, et pro isto usu, retento dominio, potest pecunia recipi; et tunc ex toto est contractus locationis vel conductionis, non autem mutuatio, sive mutui datio, et debet idem pondus in numero restituti, nisi forte sufficiat locanti
15 aequale in pondere et valore.

Hae regulae praedictae ostendunt quid iustum, quid iniustum in commutationibus statim factis, id est, quando uterque commutans statim dat vel recipit illud pro quo commutat.

[4.—NORMAE DE CONTRACTIBUS PRO FUTURO]

20 [20] Sed quando commutans non statim recipit illud pro quo commutat, sed differtur huiusmodi receptio, quaeritur quid iuris?

[DUAE REGULAE] Respondeo: praeter regulas praedictas pertinentes ad iustum et iniustum in singulis contractibus pro praesenti, addo hic duas: Prima est, quod commutans non commutet vel vendat
25 tempus, quia tempus non est suum. Secundo, quod non ponat se in tuto de lucrando, et illum cum quo commutat de damno: intelligo "in tuto" semper vel ut in pluribus.

[*Aliqui casus*] Ex istis regulis patent multi casus in speciali, verbi gratia, dicatur festum Nativitatis Domnini A, et festum sancti Ioannis
30 Baptistae B, iste commutans tradit alii rem suam in A; aut ergo tunc erat venditurus aut non, sed in B. Si sic, vel determinat nunc pretium

---

AM

1 et etiam ratione] *om.* M 2 simili] similibus A 5 istum] illud M 13 sive] sed M 14 in numero] *om.* M 17 commutans] *om.* M 20 Sed quando . . . commutat] *om.* A 21 sed] sed si A 21 quid] quis M 22 praedictas] *om.* M 24 duas] istas duas M 26 illum] istum M

[1]*Decretales Gregorii* IX, lib. V, tit. 19, cap. 19; *Corpus Iuris Canonici*, II, col. 816.
[2]Boethius, *De differentiis topicis*, lib. II (PL 94, 1090).

other things that one can loan or lease, and for this use, one can receive money while retaining the ownership. And then, the contract as a whole is one of renting or hiring and not a money loan [to be paid back with interest]. And one must restore the same numerical money–weight, unless perhaps something equal in weight or value suffices for the lender.

The aforesaid rules show what is just and what is unjust in exchanges that are made at once, that is when both the parties to the transaction immediately give or receive that for which they make the exchange.

[4.—GUIDELINES FOR CONTRACTS ABOUT FUTURES]

But when a person making the exchange does not immediately receive that for which he made the exchange, but only receives it later, what is right and just?

[TWO RULES][17] I reply: in addition to the aforesaid rules pertaining to what is just and unjust in individual contracts regarding the present, I add here these two: The first is that *the seller may not exchange or sell time*, because time does not belong to him. The second: that *he may not insure certain gain for himself at the cost of almost certain damage to the other party.* I understand this "insurance" as something that will always guarantee gain in futures or will do so most of the time.

[SOME APPLICATIONS] These rules clarify many specific cases. For example let us call the Feast of Christ's Nativity A and that of John the Baptist B and take the case of an exchange made at time A to one who intends to sell it either then, or at some time before B when he will pay for it. In this second case, the owner has two choices. Either he determines the price he is to be paid according to the article's value at time A, in which case he does the other a favor for he takes care of his neighbor's need before he is obliged to do so, namely when he gets paid at time B. Or he charges a higher price than is just at time A, and then he is guilty of usury, because he is selling time in violation of the first rule. *Decretals*, title *De Usuris*, chapter *Consuluit*[18] proves this.

But if the article was not to be sold now, but after some time when it could bring a higher price, either the owner sets a certain price for it

secundum quod tempus currit pro A, et tunc facit misericordiam, quia
tunc supplet indigentiam proximi antequam teneatur illam supplere,
quando scilicet exspectat solutionem huius usque B. Aut determinat
pretium maius quam sit iustum pro A, et tunc est usurarius, quia vendit
tempus contra primam regulam, quod probatur *Extra de Usuris,
Consuluit.*[1]

Si autem modo non esset venditurus, sed alias quando venderetur
quod secundum cursum temporis plus posset lucrari, aut ergo nunc
ponit certum pretium, aut non, sed dimittit certificationem pretii
pendentem ex aliquo futuro. Si primo modo, si ponit pretium secundum
quod res nunc valet, non est dubium quin faciat misericordiam magnam.
Si vero ponit pretium maius quam nunc valet, non tamen ita
immoderatum pretium quin tempore solutionis verisimiliter quandoque
plus, quandoque minus, valeat res vendita, ratione dubii excusatur, quia
contra nullam regulam praedictam facit, quod probatur per illud
capitulum *Naviganti*, paragrapho *Ratione*.[2]

[21] Et si obiciatur contra hoc, quia illud ibidem: In tua,[3]
respondeo: ibi continetur monitio utilis, non praeceptum necessarium.

Si autem determinationem pretii ex valore futuro illius rei
pendentem relinquat, aut ergo pro tempore determinato ut illius
solutionis, vel alio in quo consuevit regulariter res plus valere quam
quando dat rem suam, et tunc misericordiam facit; utpote concedo tibi
istud pro tanto pretio pro quanto valebit in B, vel aliquo tempore citra
B, cum tamen res consuevit communiter carior esse in B quam in aliquo
tempore praecedente.

Si autem velit pretium determinari pro tempore indeterminato hoc
modo, ut ponat se in tuto lucri ut in pluribus, et alium in damno, utpote
volo quod tantum solvas mihi pro isto quantum valebit in quocumque
tempore usque ad B, quando carius vendetur, usura est, quia ponit se,

AM

1 tempus currit] c. t. M 7 modo non esset] n. e. m. M 8 temporis] *om.* M 12 non
tamen] t. n. M | ita] *om.* M 15 nullam] add. vel neutram A 16 paragrapho] capitulo M 17
quia] per M 19 pretii] *add.* illius M 20 predentem] pendere M 21 res] *add.* ut A 22 suam]
om. M 23 istud] illud M 26 velit] *om.* A 29 quia] quando M | vel] in M

[1]*Decretales Gregorii* IX, lib. V, tit. 19, cap. 10; *Corpus Iuris Canonici*, II, col. 814.
[2]*Decretales Gregorii* IX, lib. V, tit. 19, cap. 19; *Corpus Iuris Canonici*, II, col. 816.
[3]Ibid., lib. V, tit. 19, cap. 6; *Corpus Iuris Canonici*, II, col. 813.

now, or he puts off certifying the price dependent on something in the future. Suppose he settles the matter now; if he sets the price according to value which the article has now, there is no doubt but that he does the buyer a great favor. Suppose he charges more than its present value, but not so immoderate a price that at the time it will be sold it is likely to have more or less that value. In such a case, he is excused by reason of the doubt, for he violates neither of the aforesaid rules. Proof of this is the canon *Naviganti*, paragraph *Ratione*.[19]

And if one objects against this on the basis of the canon *In tua*[20] I reply that a useful admonition is contained here, but not a necessary precept.[21]

But if he leaves the determination of the price dependent on the article's future value, then either that time is specified to be when the buyer is paid in turn for selling it, or another time is specified when the article customarily has a higher value than when he hands it over to the buyer, and then he does a favor. For instance, I give you this article for such a price as it will have at time B, or at some time beyond B when that thing will customarily be dearer than it is at time B or at any earlier time.

But it is usury if a person requires that the price be determined for some unspecified time in such a way as to guarantee almost certainly a profit for oneself and a loss for the other party; for instance, if I ask that you pay me as much for this now as it will be worth at any time up to time B when it sells for a much higher price. For then the odds are almost all in your favor with little chance of loss on your part and an almost certain loss on the part of the other who has little or nothing in his favor.

There is also another injustice here, because at some determinate day he [the buyer] will have to put his article up for sale, and not keep it until at some unspecified time [he can make a profit]. Then it will happen that he has to sell it for less than he would at any time between A and B. Consequently by such a pact, [the original seller] makes certain he gains more than he could by [his own] human industry.

The aforesaid rules then concern what is just and unjust in selling or exchanging things either for present or future delivery. Here we are speaking here of an economic transaction whereby the one making the

vel partem suam quoad lucrum ut in pluribus, et illum cum quo
contrahit ad damnum ut in pluribus; et tunc habet pro se illud quod
evenit ut in pluribus, et contra se illud quod evenit ut in paucioribus.

Est etiam alia iniustitia ibi, quia aliquo die determinato oportet eum
exponere rem suam venditori, et non in tempore particulari vago, et in
illo contingeret quod minus carius venderetur, quam in die cariori inter
A et B, et per consequens in tali pacto facit se certum de lucro ultra
quam humana industria posset pertingere.

Hae ergo regulae dictae sunt de iusto et iniusto in venditione et
commutatione quacumque pro nunc vel futuro, et hic loquendo de
commutatione oeconomica, quae est quando commutans intendit rem
accipere pro qua commutat, quia emit non ut mercetur ea, sed ut ea
utatur.

[5.—DE COMMUTATIONE OECONOMICA NEGOTIATIVA]

[22] Sequitur de commutatione negotiativa, ubi commutans intendit
mercari de re quam accipit, quia emit non ut utatur, sed ut vendat, et
hoc carius; et haec negotiativa dicitur pecuniaria vel lucrativa. De hac
ultra regulas prius positas quid iustum et quid iniustum addo duo:

[DUAE REGULAE] Primum est quod talis commutatio sit reipublicae
utilis. Secundum est quod talis iuxta diligentiam suam et prudentiam et
periculum in commutatione accipiat pretium correspondens.

[EXPLICATIO PRIMAE] Prima condicio exponitur, quia reipublicae
est utile habere conservatores rerum venalium, ut prompte possint
inveniri ab indigentibus volentibus emere. In ulteriori etiam gradu utile
est reipublicae habere afferentes res necessarias, quibus illa patria non
abundat, et tamen usus earum ibi est utilis et necessarius. Ex hoc
sequitur quod mercator, qui affert rem de patria ubi abundat ad aliam
patriam ubi deficit vel qui istam rem emptam conservat, ut prompte
inveniatur venalis a volente eam emere, habet actum utilem
reipublicae.—Hoc quoad expositionem primae condicionis.

AM
1-2 et illum...pluribus] *om.* M 2 et] it M 2 illud quod] quod M 1 vel] in M 6 cariori]
cariore M 9 Haec ergo regulae] r.e. illae M 10 hic] *om.* M 15 Sequitur] *add.* quod M 18
regulas] res A 18 positas] dictas M 21 commutatione] permutatione M 24 volentibus] *add.*
illas M 24 In ulteriori . . . gradu] om. M 1 utile] *add.* etiam M 27 qui] quia A 27 aliam] *om.*
M 1 rem] om. M 29 volente] volenti M

exchange intends to acquire the article purchased for his own use and not for resale.

[5.—RULES FOR COMMERCIAL TRANSACTIONS]

What follows are mercantile deals where the one making the exchange intends to do business with the thing he acquires, because he buys it not for his own use, but to sell it and that for a higher price; and these negotiations are called monetary or lucrative. And for such transactions, over and beyond the aforesaid rules as to what is just and unjust, I add two more.

[TWO RULES] The first is that this exchange be something that is useful for the state. The second that the price corresponds to a person's diligence, prudence and care as well as the risk one accepts in doing such business.

[EXPLANATION OF THE FIRST] The explanation for the first condition is that it is useful to the state to have suppliers who stock things for sale that they may be easily found by those wishing to buy them. Also, to go a step further, the state finds it useful to have importers of needed commodities that are scarce in the homeland, but are nevertheless beneficial or indispensable. And from this it follows that the merchant, who brings such commodities from the lands where they abound to the country where they are lacking or who stocks such imported staples for sale that they may be quickly found by one wishing to buy them, is doing business that is useful to the state.—So much for explaining the first condition.

[EXPLANATION OF THE SECOND] The second follows, for everyone engaged in honest work that serves the interests of the state *needs to live by his own labor*. I say honest, because prostitutes or charlatans live dishonestly. But this person who imports or stocks merchandise is serving the state usefully and honestly. Hence he needs to live from his labor. Nor is it this alone, but each can justly sell his industry and solicitude. The industry of one transferring things from one country to another requires a great deal; one has to consider carefully what a country may need and with what it abounds. Therefore one can justly go beyond what one needs to support oneself and one's family and,

58

[EXPLICATIO SECUNDAE] Sequitur secunda, quia unumquemque in opere honesto reipublicae servientem oportet de suo labore vivere. Honeste dixi propter meretrices et alios inhoneste viventes. Sed iste afferens vel conservans, honeste et utiliter servit reipublicae; ergo oportet eum de labore suo vivere. Nec hoc solum, sed unusquisque potest industriam et sollicitudinem suam iuste vendere: industria illius transferentis rem de patria ad patriam magna requiritur ut consideret quibus quae patria abundet et indigeat; ergo potest iuste ultra sustentationem necessariam pro se et familia sua ad istam necessitatem deputata, recipere pretium correspondens industriae suae; et ultra hoc secundo aliquid correspondens periculis suis. Ex quo enim in periculo suo transfert, est translator, vel custodit, si est custos, propter huiusmodi periculum potest secure aliquid accipere correspondens et maxime si quandoque sine culpa sua in tali servitio communitatis damnificatus est: utpote mercator transferens quandoque amisit navem onustam maximis bonis; et alius quandoque ex incendio casuali amittit pretiosissima, quae custodit pro republica.

[23] Haec omnia confirmantur, quia quantum deberet alicui ministro reipublicae legislator iustus et bonus retribuere, tantum potest ipse, si non adsit legislator, de republica sibi accipere non extorquendo. Sed si esset bonus legislator in patria indigente, deberet locare pro pretio magno huiusmodi mercatores qui res necessarias deferrent, et qui eas allatas servarent; et non tantum eis et familiae sustentationem necessariam invenire, sed etiam industriam et periculum et peritiam allocare; ergo etiam hoc possunt ipsi in vendendo.

Ex istis duabus condicionibus requisitis in negotiativa iusta patet quomodo aliqui sunt vituperabiliter negotiatores, ut scilicet illi qui nec transferunt nec conservant nec eorum industria melioratur res venalis, nec certificatur aliquis alius simplex de valore rei emendae, sed modo emit, ut statim sine omnibus istis condicionibus requisitis vendat, iste esset exterminandus a republica, vel exulandus: et vocatur ille in gallico *regratier*, quia prohibet immediatam commutationem volentium emere,

AM

2 honesto] honeste M 3 alios] istos M 3-4 iste afferens] a. i. M 4 et utiliter] *om.* M 5 labore suo] s. l. M 6 industriam] *add.* suam M | suam] *om.* M | vendere] pendere M 15 onustam] honustam M 21 deberet] debet M 22 deferrent] afferent M 24 et periculum] *om.* M | peritiam] *add.* et omnia talia M | allocare] locare M 26 condicionibus] *add.* vel conclusionibus A 27 quomodo] quando M 30 requisitis] *om.* M

estimating what is needed, one can set a price that corresponds to one's industry. Secondly, over and above this, *a person deserves something that corresponds to the danger or risk taken.* For if one is an importer, one transports things at a risk, or if one stocks things, one is at peril to guard them, and because of such dangers can securely accept some corresponding compensation; above all if, through no fault of one's own, a person suffers losses through such service to the community. For instance, a merchant shipping by sea may lose a ship loaded with most of his goods; and at other times he may through an accidental fire lose precious things he is stocking for the state.

All these matters are confirmed, for as much as a just and good legislator ought to reward any one who does a service to the state, so much can a merchant receive for himself from the state, if the legislator does not provide such, though not by extortion. In an indigent country, however, if the lawgiver is good, he ought to hire at great expense such merchants to import essential or indispensable goods and preserve and look after the things they bring. He ought to find not only the necessary sustenance for them and their families, but also make use of their industry and practical experience, and underwrite the risks they take. In offering things for sale, then, the merchants themselves can take all this into consideration.

These two conditions required for just business make clear why some businessmen deserve censure, namely those who neither import, export, conserve, improve by their industry, or set any fixed price for the value of what they offer for sale. Rather they buy up directly for immediate sale to corner the market and ignore all these conditions for doing a legitimate business. Such hucksters (the French call them *regratiers*) should be banished from the country, for they prevent the immediate exchange between buyers and those who wish to sell the goods they have imported or stocked. As a consequence, they make everything usable or salable more expensive than it should be, and of little value to the vender. Thus they harm both parties.

vel commutare oeconomice, et per consequens facit quidlibet venale vel
usuale carius ementi, quam deberet esse, et vilius vendenti, et sic
damnificant utramque partem.

[ARTICULUS III. INIUSTA OCCUPATIO ET DAMNIFICATIO ALTERIUS]

5   [24] De tertio articulo satis patet ex praedictis, quia *rectum est iudex
sui et obliqui, I *De   anima*[1] et ideo ex iustitia determinata in alio
praecedenti articulo in translationibus dominii vel usus rerum apparet
iniustitia, quae accidit in talibus, quod breviter exponi discurrendo
potest.

10   [ILLICITAE DONATIONES ET COMMUTATIONES] Nam   in
donatione non est iustitia, si donans non mere liberaliter donat, vel
contra voluntatem alicuius a quo dependet in donando, donat, sicut
patet in illo casu de quo allegatum est ibi, *Extra de censibus, Exigit*, VI
libro.[2] Non autem mere liberaliter donat si deceptus vel quasi
15   necessitate tractus donat, quia ignorantia et aliqualis coactio excludunt
voluntarium simpliciter, ex III *Ethicorum*.[3]

Ex hoc sequitur quod deceptus de eo cui donat, quantum ad illam
rationem propter quam donat non simpliciter donat; et ideo si alicui
donat tamquam propinquo, qui tamen non est propinquus, non
20   simpliciter donat.

Consimiliter, si alicui ut egeno qui non est egenus; et ideo videant
illi omnem causam, scilicet qui divites exsistentes, recipiunt tamen
tamquam egentes eleemosynas, ne iniuste omnia huiusmodi recipiant,
quia non est in dante ibi voluntarium propter condicionis ignorantiam
25   quam respicit in donando. Consimiliter, si attractus sit, ut in usuris
dandis, non est mere donatio liberalis.

Consimiliter dicendum est de accommodante licet ibi non sit
aequalis defectus propter aequale vitium, quia translatio usus ad tempus
non requirit tantam liberalitatem quantam translatio dominii.

30   [25] De permutatione est iniustita ex eisdem causis, scilicet ex

---

AM

8 in] *om.* M 8 quod] quia M 13 allegatum] allegata M | ibi] ista M 14 tractus] *add.* vel
coactus A 22 illi] *add.* scilicet M 24 ibi] *om.* M 25 si] *add.* contractus vel si A | sit] *om.* M 28
aequalis defectus] d. a. M

[1]Aristoteles, *De anima* I, t. 85, cap. 5 (411a 4-5).
[2]*Sextus Decretalium*, lib. III, tit. 20, c. 2; *Corpus Iuris Canonici*, vol. II, col 1057.
[3]Aristoteles, *Ethica Nicomachea* III, c. 1, 1111a 21-22.

[ARTICLE III. UNJUST APPROPRIATION OF PROPERTY]

As for the third article, it is clear from the foregoing, where injustice occurs, for "the straight line is the judge of both itself and the curved" (*De anima* I). And hence from the preceding article as to how justice is served as regards transfers of the ownership or the use of things it is apparent as to where injustice happens to occur. This can be shown briefly by running through the various rules.

[ILLICIT DONATIONS AND EXCHANGES] For in a donation there is no justice if the giver is not completely free or gives contrary to the will of someone upon whom he depends in giving, as is clear in that case which is cited there under the title *De censibus*, chapter *Exigit*, in *Book Six of the Decretals*.[22] But a person is not entirely free in giving if he is deceived or is forced to give by necessity, as it were. For what is done out of ignorance or under any compulsion is simply involuntary, according to Bk. III of the *Ethics*.

From this it follows that no one gives freely, in an unqualified sense, if he is deceived as to why the beneficiary should receive the gift. Hence, if a person thinks he is giving to some relative and the person is not a kinsman, he is simply not giving.

The same holds if one thinks the beneficiary is destitute whereas in reality he is not. Therefore let them examine every case, namely, where those who are rich receive donations as though they were needy, lest they receive all such contributions unjustly. For here the donor has no intention of giving because of his ignorance of the conditions which must be taken into consideration in giving. Similarly if one is forced to give as in the case of paying usurious interest, it is simply not a free donation.

The same must be said of one making a loan, although here there is not an equal defect of justice, since the transfer of the use for a period of time does not require the same liberality as the transfer of the ownership.

In exchanges [of valuables or money] there is injustice for the same reasons, namely from deception and involuntariness, as well as the [legal] prohibition of superiors. And on this last score [viz. prohibition by law], an exchange can be called unjust that takes place in games of

deceptione et involuntario, et prohibitione superioris, cui commutans subest in commutando. Et ex hoc potest dici iniusta commutatio, quae fit in ludis alearum et huiusmodi, iuxta illud ff. *de Aleatoribus*, lib. ultimo[1] et *Extra de vita et honestate clericorum, Clerici* super illud officia[2]

5 in Glossa, tamen ista lex non ligat nisi illos qui politice subsunt legi imperiali, qui forte nulli sunt hodie, quia ubi praecipue ista lex locum habere consuevit, municipialia praeiudicant imperialibus; patet ex Italia.

Iniustitiae in emptione et venditione tactae sunt prius, tangendo de iustitia in eis: et iuxta hoc de locatione et conductione ibidem patet. De

10 mutui datione et solutione iniustitia praecipua est usura, cuius vituperatio habetur *Extra de Usuris, Super eo.*[3]

[26] [CRIMEN USURAE] Usurae crimen utraque Pagina detestatur. Quod vetus, patet (Ezechiel):[4] "Ad usuram non accommodabis," etc. Quod nova, Luca 6:[5] "Date mutuum, nihil inde sperantes."

15 Et si arguitur contra hoc, quia licet unicuique in contractibus servare se indemnem, ut dictum est prius, quod vendens potest carius vendere, attendens damnum suum in vendendo, maxime si inducatur ab illo cui vendit. Ergo eodem modo si inducatur ab illo cui mutuatur, licet sibi se servare indemnem, quod non potest, nisi accipiendo aliquid ultra

20 sortem.

Similiter dans usuram, voluntarie dat, quia nullus cogit eum ad accipiendum ad usuram, sed voluntate sua accipit pecuniam, et reddit ultra sortem, et non aliter potest dominium transferre in alterum, ergo transfer dominium; ergo alius, scilicet usurarius, non habet alienum.

25 Ad primum dico quod si non vult damnificari, pecuniam sibi necessariam reservet, quia nullus eum necessitat ad faciendam

---

AM

1 involuntario] ex voluntario A 5 tamen] cum M | illos] istos M 5 politice] vivendo politice M 6 ista] illa M | consuevit] *add*. et A 7 municipialia] *add*. municipia M 9 hoc] *om*. A 10 solutione] acceptatione M 13 accommodabis] accommodabitis M | mutuum] *om*. M 15 quia] quod M 18 illo] *add*. alio M 19 se sevare] s. se M 19 nisi] *add*. in A 21 eum] *om*. M | ad accipiendum ad usuram] ad hoc M 22-23 accipit . . . sortem] *om*. M 24 dominium] *om*. M 24 scilicet] *om*. M

[1]*Digesta*, lib. XI, tit. 5 "De Aleatoribus," *Corpus Iuris Civilis* (ed. P. Krueger. Berlin: Apud Weidmannos, 1954), vol, I, p. 185.
[2]*Decretales Gregorii* IX, lib. III, tit. 1, c. 15; *Corpus Iuris Canonici*, II, col. 453.
[3]*Decretales Gregorii* IX, lib. V, tit. 19, cap. 4; *Corpus Iuris Canonici*, II, col. 812.
[4]Ezechiel 18:8.
[5]Luca 6:35.

dice and the like, according to the *Digest* and the [*Decretals*] title, *De vita et honestate clericorum*, chapter *Clerici officia*.[23] But, according to the glossator, this canon states that this only binds those living under the jurisdiction of imperial law, of which perhaps there are none today. For where imperial law was wont to apply, municipal law has replaced it, as is clear in Italy.

Injustices in buying and selling were treated earlier in discussing what justice requires in such transactions; and the same is true of injustices in lending and hiring. As for loans and their repayment, the principal injustice here is usury, whose censure is found in the *Decretals*, under the title *De Usuris*, chapter *Super eo*.[24]

[THE CRIME OF USURY] Both Testaments detest the crime of usury. That the Old Testament does is evident from Ezechiel: "If he does not lend at interest or exact usury..." As for the New Testament, there is Luke 6: "Lend without expecting repayment."

And if you argue against this that earlier we said in contracts to prevent injury to oneself, it is licit for the vender to charge more in view of what he loses by selling, especially if pressured by the buyer. By the same token, then, if someone is induced by another person to loan him money, it is lawful to provide himself indemnity. But he can only do so by accepting something more than the capital and this by a pact; otherwise he has no security.

Similarly, one accepting the money loaned does so voluntarily, for no one forces him to do this. Voluntarily, then, he takes the money and returns the capital with interest. In no other way can the money change hands except by a transfer of ownership; hence this is transferred. Therefore the first party, namely the usurer, does not have the property of another.

As to the first point, I reply that if he does not wish to be injured, he should keep the needed money to himself, for no one is bound to do a favor to his neighbor. But if he wants to do one, divine law obliges him not to vitiate the act. As for the second, although he [i.e., the debtor] transfers the ownership [of the capital plus interest], the [usurer] recipient is still bound to return [the unjust interest], just as with any money loan the ownership and use is transferred, and nevertheless the debtor is still bound to restore [the capital] to his creditor.

misericordiam proximo; sed si vult misericordiam facere, necessitatur ex
lege divina ut non faciat eam vitiatam. Ad secundum, etsi transferat
dominium, tamen recipiens tenetur restituere, sicut in mutui datione
transfertur dominium et usus, et tamen debitor tenetur tandem
restituere creditori.

[27] [NEGOTIATIONES INIUSTAE] Consimiliter patet de iniustitiis
in commutationibus, ubi fit dilatio recipiendi. Est enim iniustitia
vendendo tempus, vel se ponendo in certo de lucrando, vel simpliciter
vel ut in pluribus. Consimiliter in negotiativa est iniustitia si obsit
reipublicae actus eius, vel si immoderate recipit a republica ultra
industriam, diligentiam, sollicitudinem et pericula.

[VIOLENTA OCCUPATIO] Item, praeter istas iniustitias partiales in
istis contractibus vel commutationibus est una in iustitia generalis,
quando aliquis usurpat rem alienam domino simpliciter invito, et hoc
tam domino proximo quam remoto, scilicet legislatore, qui non vult,
immo prohibet, illam rem occupari invito domino, nisi in casibus
praescriptionis et usucapionis.

In istis autem non est translatio dominii, scilicet in furto rapina et
huiusmodi, licet sit violenta occupatio rei cuius est dominium; et ista
iniustitia manifestior est quacumque alia, ubi propter solam
defectuosam condicionem est iniustitia in translatione vel
commutatione, ut in casibus supradictis.

[ARTICULUS IV: DE OBLIGATIONE RESTITUTIONIS]

[28] De quarto articulo: primo, *propter quam rationem* sit restitutio
facienda? Secundo, *quis* teneatur restituere? Tertio, *quid*? Quarto, *cui*?
Quinto, *quando*?

[1. QUARE RESTITUTIO FACIENDA SIT?]

De primo dico quod sicut auferre alienum est mortale peccatum
contra praeceptum divinum negativum: "Non furtum facies," ita et
tenere alienum; et ideo sicut necessarium est tenere et servare praecepta
negativa, ita necessarium est non tenere alienum domino invito, et per
consequens, vel actu statim reddere, vel saltem velle reddere cum fuerit

---

AM

8 se ponendo] p. s. M 8 ut] *om.* M 12 Item] *om.* M I iniustitias] *om.* M 16 in] *om.* M
20 manifestior est] e.m. M 24 articulo] *om.* M 30 tenere alienum] a. t. M 30 tenere et] *om.*
M 32 vel actu] *om.* A I saltem] statim M

[UNJUST BUSINESS TRANSACTIONS] In like fashion, it is clear where injustices occur in credit transactions about the future, where payment is delayed. For it is not just to sell time,[25] or to insure in all or nearly all cases one's own gain and the other's loss. Similarly, there is injustice in business if the action is hurtful to the state or if a merchant receives an immoderate pay from the state in excess of what his industry, diligence, care, or risk factor warrants.

[GENERAL INJUSTICE] Besides these partial trade or contractual injustices, there is one general form of injustice that occurs when what belongs to another is taken against his will, whether the unwillingness be on the part of the proximate or remote owner, namely, the legislator who does not want, nay prohibits, that the property of another be taken over from an unwilling owner, except in cases where the ownership is acquired through long use or prescription.

Though theft, rapine, and the like involve no transfer of ownership, they forcefully seize what another owns. Here the injustice is more obvious than in those cases where the injustice stems from some illegality about the exchange or transfer of ownership, as in the cases mentioned above.

[ARTICLE IV. THE OBLIGATION OF RESTITUTION]

There are five points to be investigated regarding the fourth article. First, the reason why restitution has to be made. Second, who is bound to restitution? Third, what is one bound to restore? Fourth, to whom? Fifth, when?

[1. THE RATIONALE OF RESTITUTION]

About the first, I say that just as to rob another is a mortal sin against the divine negative precept "You shall not steal," so too it is sinful to keep what is his. As one must always observe a negative precept, so one must never keep an owner's property against his will. Hence, it must be immediately returned or at least one must intend to do so as soon as this can be done. It is not as though restitution must be made then as an integral part of general or special satisfaction, for satisfaction in general is giving the person sinned against something that

opportunitas. Unde non est restitutio facienda necessario, ut pars quaedam satisfactionis, neque generaliter accipiendo satisfactionem, neque specialiter. Generaliter enim accepta reddit pro peccato aequivalens ei, in quem peccatur; non sic ista restitutio, quia absque

5 omni redditione pro peccato posset reddi proximo quod suum est, sicut et in mutuis redditur creditori absque omni satisfactione pertinente ad reconciliationem peccatoris.

[29] Consimiliter, non est satisfactio specialis, quae est tertia pars poenitentiae, quia de congruo requiritur restitutio ante omnem partem

10 poenitentiae, sicut cessatio voluntaria in actu vel facto a peccato; sed satisfactio, quae est tertia pars poenitentiae, non requiritur ante alias duas partes poenitentiae. Immo sequitur contritionem et confessionem, ut iniuncta a sacerdote. Restitutio autem non iniungitur a sacerdote sed a lege divina. Et est simile in aliis peccatis, si teneret quis fornicariam

15 vel magis adulteram, restituere eam viro suo non est nisi cessare a peccato suo vel a transgressione huius precepti: "Non moechaberis"; et istud praecedit omnem partem poenitentiae acceptae. Et ideo sicut tenens adulteram non est capax poenitentiae, sed irrisor; et ideo veniens ad poenitentiam addit peccatum peccato, ita detinens alienum et

20 voluntate et facto, dum talis est, non est capax alicuius partis poenitentiae.

[2. QUIS TENEATUR RESTITUERE?]

[30] De secundo, *quis* tenetur, ponuntur duo versus:
Iussio, concilium, consensum, palpo, recursus.
25 *Participans, mutus, non obstans, non manifestans.*

Quorum sententia stat in hac maxima: *Quicumque abstulit vel detinet alienum, tenetur restituere.* Auferre autem potest, ut causa superior, scilicet praecipiendo; vel ut causa proxima immediate auferendo; vel ut

30 causa coadiuvans, si est socius in auferendo; vel ut causa inducens, si consulit vel favet vel adulatur tali consilio, favore vel adulatione, propter quam ablatio fit et sine qua non fieret.

Consimiliter de detinente qui immediate detinet vel cuius imperio

---

2 quaedam] quidem M 18 poenitentiae] *om.* A 18 et] *om.* A 23 quis tenetur] *om.* M 24 consensum] consensibus M 29 praecipiendo] praecise M 30 causa] *om.* M 33 detinente] detinendo M

makes up equivalently for the sin. But restitution is nothing of this sort, for one could return what belongs to one's neighbor without atoning for any sin. It is like paying back a loan to a creditor, which has nothing to do with reconciliation for sin.

Likewise restitution is not that special satisfaction that is the third part of penance. Just as in will or in deed one must cease sinning, so either in reality or in intent restitution is required *de congruo*[26] before one can perform any part of penance. But satisfaction, which is the third part of penance, is not required before the other two parts; rather it follows contrition and confession, as something imposed by the priest. Restitution, however, is not imposed by the priest, but by divine law. As with other misdeeds, if one lived in sin with a woman, one that was married, restitution to her husband is simply to cease sinning or transgressing the precept, "You shall not commit adultery," something that precedes any part of penance. One who goes on living with an adulteress is incapable of penance, but derides it, and if such a person came to receive absolution, he would only add one sin to another. So too as long as one keeps another's property both in fact and in intent, there is no possibility of performing any part of penance.

[2. WHO IS BOUND TO RESTITUTION?]

As for the second question, these two verses are cited:

> *Command, counsel, consent, cajole, comfort*
> *Partake, remain silent, allow, conceal*

A judicial statement of these ways is found in the maxim: *Whoever steals or keeps what belongs to another is bound to make restitution.* But one can cause theft, as a superior, namely by commanding it; or as a direct cause, by stealing immediately; or as a participating cause, as an accomplice in the theft; or as the cause that induces theft, if one counsels, favors, or praises the thief in such a way that without such encouragement the theft would not take place.

Likewise, a person who prevents a thief from paying back, either immediately or jurisdictionally, be it positively, primitively, or interpretatively. For instance, if one who by reason of his office has the duty to do so does not make the thief restore what he has taken, or if he

detineretur positive vel privative sive interpretative, ut scilicet quia non facit restitui cum ei ex officio hoc competeret, vel auxilium vel favorem praebendo, ut si tacet requisitus in iudicio, ubi sententialiter posset res restitui domino suo, et tamen dicendo veritatem, non imminet sibi
5 periculum status vel personae.

Unde breviter, omnis obligatio ad restitutionem reducitur ad auferre vel detinere, et hoc vel ut causa principalis, vel ut proxima, vel coadiuvans, vel inducens, vel non impediens, quando eius impeditio esset ad bonum reipublicae, et sine periculo personae impeditae.

10 Et haec omnia, ex quo reducuntur ad consensum efficacem, verum vel interpretativum. Probatur per illud 2 q. 1, *Notum sit*,[1] ubi dicitur *"quod facientem et consentientem par poena constringit."* Et hoc accipitur a priori ex dicto Pauli ad Romanos 2:[2] "Non solum qui talia agunt, sed etiam qui consentiunt facientibus."

15 Istorum omnium quilibet tenetur ad restitutionem in solidum; sed uno restituente omnes alii liberantur a debito in comparatione ad illum damnificatum; tamen alii tenetur pro rata portionis, quae eos contingit, illi qui pro omnibus satisfecit.

[3. Quid Restituendum est?]

20 [31] De tertio, *quid*, dico quod non solum ad restituendum rem ablatam vel usum rei, sed etiam ad interesse ut fructum perceptum de re, si res erat fructifera, tenetur, sed non fructum qui provenit ex industria eius qui utitur illa re. Ex quo sequitur quod lucrum requisitum de pecunia foenebri non tenetur foenerator reddere; alioquin ille qui
25 reciperet, posset iuste esse usuarius, quia recipere fructum de sua pecunia, provenientem per industriam alterius, est facere usuram. Et illud est forte quod magis posset inducere homines ad usuram, quia de usuris lucrantes, illud quod lucrantur non tenetur restituere; immo illud

---

AM

3 sententialiter posset] p. s. M | res] *om.* A 6 Unde] Vel M 7 ut] de M 7 ut] *om.* M | vel non] et non M 9 impeditae] impedire M 13 ex dicto] et e dicto M 13 ad] secundum M | solum] *add.* eos M | etiam] *om.* M 16 illum] alium M 17 portionis] portione A 20 quid dico quod] respondeo M 21 ut] *om.* A 23 requisitum] exquisitum M 24 foenerator reddere] restituere A 27 illud] istud M 27 inducere homines] h. i. M

[1]*Decretum Gratiani*, Secunda pars, causa 2, q. 1, c. 10; *Corpus Iuris Canonici*, I, col. 443.
[2]Rom. 1:32.

abets or favors such a refusal, or keeps quiet in a court of law where a judicial sentence could force the delinquent to restore the property to its owner, and nevertheless if he told the truth, there would be no danger to his own person or reputation.

To put it briefly, every obligation to restitution is reducible to taking property away or preventing its return, and this either as a principal cause or as the direct or proximate cause or as a collaborator or instigator or not preventing it when this would contribute to the public welfare and would not harm the person kept from making restitution.

And all these, which come down to efficacious consent, either in truth or by interpretation, are proved through that canon *Notum sit*, where it is said *"the perpetrator and the one consenting to it are bound equally to restitution."* And this we gather from what St. Paul says in his epistle to the Romans that not only are those guilty who do such things but those who approve of them in others.

And each one as part of the group has an obligation to make restitution. But if one of them makes restitution, all the others are freed from their obligation so far as damage to the owner is concerned; nevertheless the others are held to make recompense according to their share of the guilt to the person who makes satisfaction for the group as a whole.

[3. WHAT IS ONE BOUND TO RESTORE?]

As for the third, namely the "what," I say that not only is one bound to restore the property, or the use of the thing, but also the interest and the fruit, if it is fruit bearing—but not such fruit as results from the industry of the person who used it.[27] From which it follows that a capitalist is not bound to return the requisite profit on the money he has loaned or invested.[28] Otherwise he who borrowed or received the money could licitly be a usurer, for to receive the fruit of his money coming from the industry of another is to practice usury. (And perhaps this is what could be the greatest incentive for men to practice usury. For those who make a profit as money lenders are not bound to restore that which they make as a profit.) Indeed this is the lender's own, for it is acquired through his industry. If that from which the profit came was

suum est quia per industriam suam adquisitum. Si idem de quo adquisivit erat etiam alienum vel alii, iuste restituendum.

[4. CUI RESTITUTIO FACIENDA SIT?]

[32] De quarto, *cui*, dico quod damnificato, si tamen sit possibile, "possibile"—inquam—ut si novit eum, vel si habet eum praesentem vel habere potest ut sibi mittatur sine maiori incommodo quam illud quod mittendum est esset utile ei cui mittitur. Et intelligo de ipso vel de aliquibus eius propinquis, si mortuus sit vel absens, quia praesumitur lege naturae quod ille magis velit restitutionem fieri propinquis suis. Et ideo in duobus casibus, nec illi nec suis, utpote si nescitur cui; vel scito cui tamen, mortuo et nesciuntur propinqui eius. In alio casu si maiores sumptus essent ponendi in mittendo quam illud valeat illi cui illud mittitur. Si quaeras in istis: cui? dico quod pauperibus vice huius, quia cui non potest temporaliter reddi, redditur spiritualiter; redditio spiritualis fit maxime reddendo pauperibus pro illo.

Si quaeras per manus cuius debet reddi pauperibus? Respondeo: non inveni quis necessario determinatus sit mediator in distribuendo ista pauperibus. Dicit unus doctor quod confessor vel aliquis de cuius fidelitate credat. Videtur mihi quod per seipsum. Cum consilio tamen alicuius boni viri potest istud distribuere pauperibus, quia tali mediatori posset dari ut restitueret, de cuius fidelitate praesumeret, et tamen iste sibi ipsi applicaret vel aliis usibus quam deberet. Unde ubi lex divina vel ecclesiastica non ligat personam, sequenda est ratio naturalis. Illa autem dictat quod persona quae tenetur magis restituat pauperibus per seipsam quam per aliam, licet non excludendo consilium alicuius boni viri sed includendo.

[5. QUANDO RESTITUTIO FACIENDA SIT?]

[33] De quinto, *quando*, dico non licet aliquo tempore detinere alienum invito domino, id est, nec volente, et secundum rectam

---

AM

1 industriam suam] s. i. M | si idem . . . adquisivit] *om.* M in mg. A 2 erat etiam] etiam e. M 2 vel] et M 5 eum praesentem] *om.* M 6 quam] quod M 8 sit] est M | vel] quod si M | absens] *add.* est M 9 restitutionem] *add.* rei M 10 vel] etiam M 12 cui illud] cui M 13 Si quaeras in istis] Et in istis si q. M 13-cui] *add.* dabo A | quod] *om.* M | huius] illius M 22 ipsi] *om.* M 24 seipsam] *add.* magis M 28 dico] respondeo M 29 id est] *om.* A | nec volente] nolente M

the property of another or belonged to another,[29] it must in justice be returned.

[4. TO WHOM MUST RESTITUTION BE MADE?]

As for the fourth, namely, to whom should restitution be made, I say it should be to the party injured. But—I add—if it is possible to do so, for instance if one knows who that party is, and if he is or could be reached, for example, if it could be sent to him without such great inconvenience as would outweigh its use to the party to whom it is sent. And I understand this either of the person himself, or his relatives, if he be dead or has gone away. For by the law of nature it is presumed that he would want it to be given rather to his relatives. There are two cases where you may well ask: To whom should I make restitution? One is if the owner is unknown, or he is known to be dead and his relatives are unknown. The other is if it costs more to send it than it would be worth to the recipient. And if you ask in such cases to whom should restitution be made? I say: to the poor in his place, because one to whom temporal restitution cannot be made, may be paid back spiritually, especially by giving alms to the poor for him.

And if you ask, through whose hands should it be given to the poor? I reply that I have found no specific party who has to mediate this distribution to the poor. One doctor claims it should be the confessor or some one he thinks reliable. It seems to me he should give it himself. With the advice of some good man, however, he could distribute it to the poor. For a mediator presumed to be dependable might apply it to himself or put it to uses other than he ought. Hence, where divine or church law does not bind a person, natural reason should be followed. But this dictates that the person who holds the property should restore it to the poor himself rather than through another, although the advice of another good man should not be excluded but included.

[5. WHEN MUST RESTITUTION BE MADE?]

As for the fifth question, namely, when should restitution be made, I say that it is not licit at any time to retain the property of another when the owner is unwilling. By "unwilling" I mean that according to

72

rationem nolle debente, et per consequens, regulariter restitutio facienda est statim, sicut statim cessandum est ab actu cuiuscumque peccati mortalis, non tantum exteriori, sed interiori.

Sed in casibus talibus quandoque licet differe restitutionem exteriorem, posita tamen interiori, scilicet voluntate restituendi cum occurrerent circumstantiae opportunae. Illi autem casus universaliter continentur sub hac maxima: *Licet detinere rem alienam quando ille debet velle rationabiliter eam detineri.* Sed in quibusdam casibus hoc velle debet aliquis rationabiliter, scilicet rem suam detineri ab alio de facto, posita iam restituendi voluntate cum circumstantiis opportunis.

Debet enim velle quilibet restitutionem sibi non fieri tunc quando est in praeiudicium communitatis, vel ipsius recipientis restitutionem, quia debet velle bonum suum et bonum commune et ita dilationem aliqualem illius restitutionis boni utilis ut servetur bonum maius.

Debet etiam tunc non velle fieri restitutionem quando est in praeiudicium et infamationem restituentis, quia debet magis velle famam proximi quam illud modicum commodum suum et hoc statim. Similiter debet magis velle quod vitetur magnum incommodum proximi restituentis, quam modicum incommodum suum vel nullum in illa modica dilatione restituentis.

Ex his sequitur quod quando esset restitutio damnosa reipublicae vel ei cui fit vel diffamativa restituentis vel nimis notabiliter damnosa tunc non tenetur ad statim restituendum, sed sufficit quod statim ex affectu restituat et quod actu restituat cessantibus inconventibus hinc et inde.

[34] Si obicitur: restituere est actus praecepti negativi, quia non tenere alienum; ad observationem autem praecepti negativi tenetur quilibet semper et pro semper; respondeo: tenere alienum iniuste, id est, invito domino, est semper prohibitum, et ideo semper et pro semper oportet non tenere isto modo. Sed quando aliquis habet voluntatem restituendi pro tempore oportuno, ex tunc tenet domino volente, etsi non actu elicito, tamen actu debito, quia dominus debet velle, quod qui suum habeat, teneat quousque possit reddere opportune.

AM

2 est statim] s. e. M 2 cessandum est] e. c. M 6 occurrerent] *add.* opportunitas vel A 10 cum] *om.* M 14 bonum maius] m. b. M 15 tunc non velle] v. t. n. M | fieri restitutionem] r. f. M 18 Similiter] Consimiliter M 18 magnum] *om.* M 19 vel nullum] *om.* M 23 tunc] *om.* M | ad statim] s. a. M 24-25 et inde] i. e. M

right reason he does not, nor should not, want it to be kept. Hence the general rule is that it should be restored at once, just as one should immediately desist from any act of mortal sin, whether it be external or internal.

But sometimes there are cases where it is legitimate to put off making external restitution, presupposing however that there is an interior will to do so when opportune circumstances occur. These cases are contained under this maxim: *It is lawful to retain the property of another when the person to whom it belongs would reasonably wish it to be retained.* But there are certain cases where someone ought to reasonably want this, namely that his property in fact be retained by the other, granted that this party already has the will to restore it when the circumstances are opportune.

For no one should want restitution made to him when it is not in his best interests or that of the community. For he should desire both his own and the common good, and so regard some delay in the restitution of his property as useful, since it serves a greater good.

Neither should he want restitution to be made when it would result in the defamation of the one making it, for he should desire the good name of his neighbor more than the minor inconvenience he suffers at present. Nor should he want his neighbor to go to great trouble to make restitution when he suffers little or no discomfort from the delay.

From this it follows that when restitution is harmful to recipient or the state, or defames the person making restitution, or entails too little significant damage, one is not bound to make restitution at once. It is enough if one immediately has the intention to do so, and actually makes restitution when this or that inconvenience no longer exists.

And if one objects that to restore is an act of a negative commandment, and the observation of a negative precept obliges *semper et pro semper*, I reply that to hold the property of another unjustly, that is, where the owner is unwilling, is always prohibited and therefore *semper et pro semper*. But once one has the will to restore it when an opportunity comes, from that moment on he holds it by the will of the owner, although not by an elicited act on his part. For the owner should wish that his property be kept until it could be opportunely given back.

74

Quod si dicas: dominus hic est invitus, quia non vult quod per quantumcumque tempus teneatur suum, respondeo quod domino male et inordinate volente statim rehabere suum, et per consequens inordinate nolente proximum suum illud tenere, non est tenens iniustus, quia etiam depositum de cuius redditione semper lex strictissima est, potest teneri licite domino invito voluntate inordinata.

Et ad istam particulam "quando" possunt reduci multi alii casus a praedictis. Unus specialis est qui etiam potest reduci ad primam particulam "quis," scilicet quando ablatio fuit occulta, tunc non tenetur ablator se prodere nec per consequens per seipsum restituere, sed per personam aliam secretam et fidelem. Et expedit quod per confessorem, quia sibi est crimen detectum in confessione et de eius fidelitate quod restituat fidei suae commissum satis debet credi; potest igitur hic differri restitutio quousque voluntas talis personae et opportunitas habeatur.

Alius etiam casus quando potest differi reddere qui etiam posset reduci ad "quis." Quando enim est impotens, pro tunc non tenetur, tamen tenetur post cum pervenerit ad pinguiorem fortunam, sicut probatur *Extra de Solutionibus, Odoardus;*[1] sicut etiam in Glossa notatur quod illa actio non exspirat per inopiam debitoris, sed sopitur; unde illud: *Inanis est actio quam excludet inopia debitoris.* Sed ius agendi manet sicut obligatio in debitore, licet sopita.

[AD ARGUMENTA PRINCIPALIA]

[35] Ad argumenta principalia: [Ad 1] Ad primum patet ex prima particula ultimi articuli *propter quam rationem,* quia non ad restitutionem ut ad satisfactionem proprie dictam, quae est tertia pars poenitentiae; sed tenetur ad eam ut ad cessationem a peccato; et hoc actu et effectu cum circumstantiis debitis et opportunis.

[Ad 2] Ad secundum et tertium patet ex dictis in tertio articulo, quia nesciens tenetur reddere pauperibus. Sed quod adducitur de nescientia domini rei inventae, dico quod res inventa debet tradi alicui personae publicae custodienda, et in locis publicis proclamari, ut sic dominus qui

---

AM

5 semper lex] l. s. M 15 differi] *om.* M 15 etiam] *om.* M 17 ad] *add.* uberiorem sive A 21 sicut] *add.* et M 23 principalia *om.* M 1 ex] in M 24 ultimi articuli] a. u. M 26 effectu] *add.* vel forte affectu A 27 et] vel M 28 dictis] praedictis M 1 tertio] secundo M

[1]*Decretales Gregorii* IX, lib. III, tit. 23, cap. 3; *Corpus Iuris Canonici,* II, col. 532.

If you say, the owner is unwilling, because he does not wish that his property be held for any length of time, I reply that the owner has a wicked and inordinate will if he does not want his neighbor to retain the property that belongs to himself. Neither does that neighbor retain it unjustly. For a deposit that even the most strict law obliges one to return, can be retained licitly if the owner's will to have it back is inordinate.

Many cases other than those just cited can be listed under the question "when." There is one special case that could also be put under the heading of "who" or "to whom," namely, when the theft was occult. For then the thief is not required to betray himself, nor, as a consequence, make restitution personally, but rather through some other discreet person. This can readily be carried out by the confessor, since in his case the crime has been detected in confession and one ought to trust in his dependability to restore what is committed to him in faith. Hence, one can put off making restitution until a person willing to do this can be found and has the opportunity to do so.

Another case of "when" restitution could be deferred could also be put under "who." For when one is simply unable at present to make restitution, one is not bound. But such persons are still obligated to repay later if their personal fortune improves, as is proved from the canon on *Odoardus*, under the title *De solutionibus*.[30] And the Glossator also notes that this obligation for repayment does not expire with the inability of the debtor to pay, but is merely suspended. Hence the judgment: "Void is the action that excludes the indigence of the debtor." But the right to take action as well as the obligation of the debtor remains, though in abeyance.

[REPLY TO THE INITIAL ARGUMENTS]

[TO 1] The answer to the first of the initial arguments is clear from the first part of the last article as to the reason why a person is not bound to restitution, as if this entailed satisfaction proper, which is the third part of penance. But he is bound to restitution in the same way as he has to stop sinning, and he is required to actually make restitution in reality when the circumstances are appropriate and opportune.

eam amisit possit ad eam pertingere. Sed si post talem proclamationem nullus dominus appareat, faciendum est sicut de restitutione vaga.

[Ad 3] Ad aliud patet quod non est maior sumptus ponendus in missione quam valeat illud quod mittitur, sed exspectanda est praesentia personae, si quandoque credatur haberi vel si non credatur haberi, nec nuntius interveniat sine nimis sumptibus, tradendum est parentibus, qui si non adsint, dandum est pauperibus. Universaliter enim dando eleemosynam pauperibus pro aliquo, datur illi bonum spirituale, et in hoc fit sibi restitutio possibilis, quando non potest sibi bonum temporale reddi.

[Ad 4] Ad aliud, si persona occupans rem alienam sit multum necessaria reipublicae, et esset in necessitate arcta, et illa persona cui debetur, similiter, argumentum haberet aliquam evidentiam. Sed de hoc dicetur statim in responsione ad secundum argumentum. Sed si illud iniuste detentum a persona multum necessaria reipublicae, non sit sibi necessarium simpliciter, sed tantum ad salvandum statum suum solemnem, dico quod non licet alicui statum suum solemnem tenere de bonis alienis, nec tantum valet reipublicae istius status solemnis quem tenet per non restitutionem quantum valet iustitia et fidelitas eius et iustitia communis.

[36][Ad 5] Ad aliud: aut detinens est in extrema necessitate, et ille cuius res est, non, sed habet aliquam citra extremam necessitatem, et tunc dicendum quod ista res fit detinentis "iure poli, quo in extremae necessitatis articulo ad providendum sustentationi naturae, via omnibus extrema necessitate detentis est concessa," *Extra de Verborum significatione, Exiit qui seminat*, et est hodie in *Sexto libro Decretalium*.[1]

Si autem ambo, scilicet detinens et ille cuius res detinetur, sunt in extrema necessitate, si prius devenit dominus ad istam necessitatem quam detinens, debet reddi domino duplici iure: tum quia prius suum, tum quia iam ex ista necessitate factum est suum. Si vero prius detinens devenit ad istam extremam necessitatem, factum est suum, et tunc domino postea devenienti ad istam necessitatem, non debet reddi, quia

---

AM

2 nullus dominus] d. n. M 11 aliud] quintum A 12 illa] alia M 16 tantum] om. M 18 alienis] alterius M 19 iustitia et fidelitas] f. e. i. M 21 aliud] sextum A 23 dicendum] dico M | fit add. istius M 25-26 Verborum significatione] s. v. M 28 istam] extremam M | debet] oportet M 29 domino] om. M 32 istam] om. M

[1]*Sextus Decretalium*, lib. V, tit. 12, c. 1; *Corpus Iuris Canonici*, II, col. 1113.

The [fourth] article provides an answer to the second and third arguments. [TO 2] For one, ignorant of the party to whom restitution is due, is bound to give to the poor. As for what is brought up there about finding a lost article of unknown ownership, I say that such a thing should be given to some public guardian and kept in a public place where the owner could reclaim it. But after it is put up for claim, if no owner appears, it must be treated like the case where there is no definite person to whom restitution must be made.[31]

[TO 3] To the other argument, it is evident that it must not cost more to send the property to be restored than it is worth. But one must look for someone present to give it to when this can be done. If one believes this cannot be done nor a messenger be sent without too much trouble, it must be given to the parents or, if they are not there, then to the poor. For generally speaking, giving alms to the poor for someone is giving that person a spiritual benefit, and in this way restitution can be made when it is impossible to return a temporal good to that person.

[TO 4] As for the other argument, if the person of greater necessity to the state, who keeps another's property, is in dire necessity and the other person to whom it is owed is in like straits, then the argument would seem to have some validity. The answer to such a case is to be found in the reply to the next argument. But if what is unjustly detained by a person of great importance to the state is not needed in any unqualified sense, but is only necessary to preserve his lofty reputation, I claim it is not licit for anyone to retain his solemn status by holding the property of others, nor is his standing by not making restitution of such value to the state as to outweigh its own fidelity and communal justice.

[TO 5] To the other, either the one retaining it is in extreme necessity and the person to whom it belongs is not, (although he is in some need of it, it is less than extreme); and then it must be said that this thing becomes the property of the detainer by reason of his right to live (*jus poli*). This right to provide what is needed to sustain one's nature is a way conceded to everybody in extreme necessity and is cited in the article about dire need in *Exiit qui seminat*, found under the title *De Verborum significatione*, which today is *in Book Six of the Decretals*.[32]

But if both are in extreme necessity, namely the detainer and the person whose property is being held, if it was the original owner who

cessavit dominium eius in re ista, et actum est alterius iure poli. Si autem ambo simul deveniant, dico quod debet reddi domino, quia ille nunquam decidit a dominio.

Et si arguas: magis debet quilibet diligere se quam proximum suum
5 et per consequens magis vitam suam corporalem quam proximi, et per consequens istam rem simpliciter necessariam sibi retinere quam dare proximo, respondeo: Magis debet diligere vitam suam ordinate, ut est diligibilis ad vitam aeternam, et ita magis conservationem iustam vitae suae, quam conservationem vitae proximi sui. Sic enim debet latro
10 magis sustinere suspendium quam occidere suspendentem, ut evadat. Cuius ratio est quia dilectio vitae corporalis iniuste custoditae non est dilectio ordinata, quia non est ad dilectionem animae nec Dei. Istius autem detinentis, in casu ultimo custoditio vitae de re aliena est iniusta, et cum hoc etiam est homicida, quia iniuste occidit alium qui subtrahit
15 sibi necessarium quod sibi debetur.

Sed numquid post extremam necessitatem, si deveniat detentor in primo vel secundo casu ad pinguiorem fortunam, tenetur tunc reddere? Videtur quod sic, quia illa est de impossibilitate, sicut allegatum est supra *De solutionibus, Odoardus.*[1]

20 [37] Contra: res illa facta est illius detinentis per hoc quod fuit in extrema necessitate, et per consequens desinit esse domini primi. Igitur non esset sibi reddenda.—Posset dici quod res talis necessaria simpliciter non posset esse nisi aliquid pertinens ad victum, et tunc consumeretur et iuste, quia ille consumens fuit dominus. Tenetur tamen
25 post, deveniens ad pinguiorem fortunam, reddere aequivalens, quia obligatio ad aequivalens videtur ortum habuisse per comparationem ad illam occupationem primam rei alienae, quae fuit iniusta ante extremam necessitatem, et ideo illa obligatio per extremam necessitatem non est extincta, sed sopita. Sed si numquam ante extremam nececessitatem
30 occupasset, tunc iuste occupasset, et ut rem suam, nec ad aliquam tenetur restitutionem.

[Ad 6] Ad illud de gladio patet ex quando in 3° articulo.

[38] [Ad 7] Ad illud de adultera dicitur multipliciter. Uno modo

AM

4 arguas] add. quia M | quam] add. vitam M 6 sibi] add. magis M 21-22 Igitur . . . reddenda] om. A 25 ad] om. M 30 iuste] add. simpliciter M | ut] om. M 32 Ad illud] om. M

[1]*Decretales Gregorii* IX, lib. III, tit. 23, cap. 3; *Corpus Iuris Canonici*, II, col. 532.

first fell into such dire need, what is his must be returned to him by a twofold right. Both because it first was his, and because he already has a claim on it by reason of his need. If however it was the detainer who first fell into dire need, and afterwards the owner did the same, he ought not to return it, since the original owner lost his right to it when it became the property of the detainer by the *jus poli*. But if both fell into such need at the same time, I say it ought to be returned to the owner because he never lost his right to it.

And if you argue that one should love oneself more than neighbor, and hence, the detainer should love his own life more than that of his owner, I reply: He should love his own life more, but only in an orderly fashion, as it is able to be loved with a view to eternal life. Thus he should love more a just conservation of his own life than conserving the just life of his neighbor. But an unjust conservation of his life is not to be preferred to a just conservation of his neighbor's life. That is why a thief ought to suffer hanging rather than kill the one hanging him to escape dying himself. The reason for this is that the love of one's bodily life preserved unjustly is not an orderly love, since it not ordered to the love of one's soul nor to the love of God. But in the last case the preservation of the life of the detainer through the possession of another's property is unjust, and murder is also coupled with this, for he is unjustly killing the person by taking from him a necessity that belongs to him.

But after the extreme necessity has passed, and the detainer in the first or second case has had the good fortune to become more affluent, is he then not bound to restitution? The rule seems to be that he is, for it is about the impossibility discussed above about the canon *Odoardus* in *De solutionibus*.[33]

To the contrary, what was taken had become the property of the detainer on the basis of his dire need and consequently the ownership of the first party had ceased. Hence it should not be restored to him.—One could reply that it could not be absolutely necessary unless it was something like food, and then it would have been consumed and justly so, for one becomes the owner of what is licitly eaten. But after he has come into more fortunate circumstances, he still has to restore something equivalent, for the obligation to return the equivalent seems

quod ipsa debet revelare peccatum suum filio suo spurio et inducere eum ad dimittendum haereditatem vero haeredi propter hoc quod iniuste occupat eam, quia non est sua. Aliter dicitur, quod minus valet, quod debet revelare culpam suam marito, ut assignet haereditatem vero haeredi: quod licitum est secundum Iura imperialia, ubi testans primo in testamento instituit haeredem.

Contra primam responsionem, quia aut filius crederet matri aut non: si autem crederet, non est probabile quod propter hoc dimitteret haereditatem, quia pauci inveniuntur ita perfecti ut propter iustitiam servandam in foro Dei, dimittant magnas possessiones quas possunt tenere iure exteriori, nec hoc etiam potest mater praesumere nisi multum prius experta fuisset voluntatem filii sui. Non autem debet se exponere certo periculo diffamationis apud filium suum propter incertam correctionem filii. Si vero non crederet, tunc essent duo mala, quia ipsa esset diffamata, et ipse teneret haereditatem, ut prius.

Contra secundam responsionem arguitur, quia mulier se diffamat et exponit se periculo mortis et maritum periculo uxoricidii, quia talis posset esse zelator, ut sunt multi qui illam occiderent vel saltem perpetuo haberent odio, et a se et ab actu coniugii expellerent. Ad ista autem mala diffamationis, mortis, vel saltem odii vel discordiae, quae sunt valde probabilia, et videntur ut in pluribus eventura, non debet mulier se exponere propter incertum bonum haereditatis restituendae. Et praeter hoc in terris ubi primogenitus universaliter est haeres, pater si crederet uxori, non posset a spurio auffere haereditatem nisi in foro publico probaret eam talem, et tunc oporteret mulierem diffamari, non tantum apud maritum, sed apud totam patriam.

[39] Dico ergo quod mulier debet laborare quantum potest ad hoc ut haereditas reddatur vero haeredi. Quantum in se est, dico, quia non debet se diffamationi exponere, sed ex aliis causis honestis filium spurium quantum potest inducere ut dimittat haereditatem. Unus modus honestus est ut intret religionem; alius ut fiat clericus et recipiat beneficia ecclesiastica, et his quasi suffficientibus contentus, haereditatem dimittat alii fratri quasi laico remanenti.

AM

1 revelare] add. casum suum sive A I suo] om. M 3 iniuste occupat] o. i. M I eam] om. M I quia] quod M 5 quod] quia M 7 matri] om. M 15 ipsa esset] etiam ipsa M 18 esse zelator] z. e. M I qui] quod M 18 vel] add. quod M I perpetuo] om. A 19 ista] illa M 20 saltem] om. M 23 pater] patris M 25-26 non tantum . . . patriam] om. M 29 debet] oportet M 31 est] om. M 32 beneficia ecclesiastica] e. b. M

to stem from the fact that before his extreme need ever arose, his initial retention of what belonged to another was unjust, and his extreme necessity did not extinguish his obligation but only put it temporarily to rest. Had he never seized what he did before his dire need arose, he could then have justly taken it as his own and would have had to make restitution to no one.

[TO 6] To the other point about the sword, the answer is evident from what was said about *when* restitution must be made in the [fourth] article.[34]

[TO 7] To the argument about the adulteress several answers are given. One claims she should reveal her crime to her bastard son to induce him to return to the true heir the patrimony he has no right to possess, since it is not his. Another answer, of lesser value, is that she should reveal her fault to her husband, that he may assign the inheritance to the true heir. This was licit according to imperial law, where the one making a last will indicated in the first place his heir.

The first reply is no good, because her son would either believe or not believe his mother. If he did believe her, he probably would not be willing to give up the heritage. Few individuals are found to be so perfect that in God's forum they would renounce great possessions which they could retain according to the external law; nor could the mother presume he would do so unless she had a great deal of prior knowledge of the mind of her son. But she ought not to expose herself to the certain danger of defamation because of the uncertain compensation her son might make. And if he did not believe her, then two evils would result, for she would be defamed and he would retain the estate, as before.

Against the second reply is this argument. Not only would a woman besmirch herself but she would expose herself to the threat of death and her husband to the sin of uxoricide. For the man could well be a zealot, as many are who either kill the wife or at least forever hate her, avoiding her company and refusing her the conjugal act. For the uncertain good that the inheritance would be restored, the woman should not expose herself to these evils of defamation, death, or at least hatred or discord, all of which are highly probable, and would almost invariably take place. And besides this, in countries where the firstborn is the heir, the father,

Si vero per nullam honestam persuasionem potest mater flectere cor filii spurii ut dimittat haereditatem, non videtur quod debeat se prodere illi spurio, quia non est certa quod talis sic impersuasibilis ab ipsa in aliis honestis, propter istud flecteretur. Immo forte teneret
5 tenacius, concipiens dimissionem esse in diffamationem sui, quia per illam notaretur esse spurius et talem notam multum cavent male nati. Et tunc mater debet laborare aliunde restitutionem fieri vero haeredi quantum potest, et secundum correspondentiam iustitiae, quia non dico quod teneatur ad restituendum aequivalens toti haereditati, nam
10 multum distat inter habere et prope esse. Iste autem numquam habuit haereditatem, licet prope fuerit secundum iustitiam, et ideo minus quam aequivalens sufficit sibi pro restitutione, et illud minus determinetur secundum arbitrium boni viri. Videtur tamen ad minus quod debeat sibi providere de victu honesto et vestitu, si fuit haereditas ita pinguis ut
15 possit sufficere haeredi ad duplum vel ad triplum istius. Quod si nec hoc possit, est in illo capitulo *Odoardus*.[1]

[40] [Ad 8] Ad ultimum[2] similiter, quod ille tenetur restituere beneficium non totum, quia multum interest inter habere et prope esse, sed aliquam portionem correspondentem alicui parti valoris beneficii.
20 Et hoc si directe abstulit sibi beneficium intentione damnificandi eum. Si autem indirecte, scilicet procurando sibi ipsi et cum hoc damnificare alium intendendo nec alias pecasset, tenetur, ut prius dixi. Sed si tantummodo propriae utilitati intendebat providere, et sic procuret sibi, et ex consequenti alius praeter intentionem istius damnificatur, ille ad
25 nihil tenetur isti, quia licet cuique sibi ipsi providere, alio neglecto.

Confirmatur istud per illud ff. *De novi operis nunciatione*, lege secunda:[3] si praescindo venas in fundo meo per quas derivabatur aqua ad puteum alterius, in intentione nocendi sibi, teneor sibi ad restitutionem damni. Sed si hoc facio sine fraude, intendens consulere utilitati et

---

AM
1 Si] Et si M I vero] om. M I persuasionem] add. unde M 1 mater] om. M 2 debeat se] s. d. M 3 quod] quia M 4 istud] illud M I flecteretur] non flecteretur M 5 esse in diffamationem] om. M 10 autem numquam] n. a M 13 ad minus] om. M 16 illo capitulo] c. i. M 22 intendendo] intendebat M I prius] om. M 25 isti] illi M 26 istud] idem M 29ff et necessitati] om. M

[1]*Decretales Gregorii* IX, lib. III, tit. 23, cap. 3; *Corpus Iuris Canonici*, II, col. 532.
[2]Codex A (f. 235va) notat in margine: "Istud non est supra argutum."
[3]*Digesta*, lib. 39, tit. 3, nn. 11-12 "Idem aiunt," in *Corpus Iuris Civilis*, vol. I, p. 645. 4 Ibid., lib. 50, tit. 17, n. 151, p. 924.

if he were to believe his wife, could not take the inheritance from her firstborn bastard unless he proved in the public forum that he was illegitimate, and then his wife would have to lose her good name not only in the eyes of her husband but of the whole land.

Therefore, I say that the woman should try as far as she can to restore the inheritance to the true heir insofar as it is in her power to do so. I say, in her power, for she ought not lay herself open to infamy, but try as far as she can to induce her illegitimate son for honorable reasons to renounce his patrimony. One respectable way would be for him to enter the religious state; another would be to become a cleric and receive an ecclesiastical benefice, and sufficiently content with this, as it were, he may give the inheritance to his other brother who remains a layman.

But if the mother cannot change the bastard's heart to renounce his heritage by any upright means, it does not seem she should inform him, since she has no assurance that one who was so far unpersuadable would be influenced by such a disclosure. Perhaps, in fact, he would hang on more tenaciously, thinking his renouncement would disgrace him, because by giving it up he would be recognized as a bastard. Those misbegotten take great care to avoid such notoriety. And then the mother would have to strive in other ways to make restitution to the true heir insofar as she can and in accord with some measure of justice. For I do not say she is bound to restore the equivalent of the entire inheritance, since there is a great difference between possessing something and being close to having it. But this son never gets his inheritance but only something approximating it in justice. Hence, something less than its full value suffices for restitution in her case, and this lesser amount is determined according to the judgment of a prudent man. But it seems that the disfranchised son he should be provided with a respectable state of life including apparel, at the very least, and two or three times that much if the inheritance was sumptuous. But if this is not possible, then her situation is to be treated like that described in that canon *Odoardus*.[35]

And finally[36] a like solution holds for [one who deprives another of a benefice]. Since the difference between having and nearly having is great, he is bound to restore not the entire benefice, but a part of its

necessitati propriae, ut quia utile est mihi facere murum, qui non potest convenienter fundari sine praecisione illarum venarum, non damnifico alium, quia ius habeo faciendi utilitatem meam in fundo meo. Et ff. *De regula Iuris*:[1] "Nemo damnum facit nisi qui illud facit quod facere ius non habet." Iste autem habet ius procurandi sibi beneficium, servatis circumstantiis iustis et honestis.

---

[1]*Ibid.*, lib. 50, tit. 17, p. 924.

value. And this if he stole the benefice directly to hurt the other; indirectly, however, if he wanted both the benefice and injury to the other, but no other sin, he is bound as I said above. But if he only wanted to provide for his own needs and thus acquired the benefice for himself and with no thought of harming another, he is not bound to any restitution, for each person can lawfully provide for his own needs without having to look to another's.

Civil Law confirms this, under the title *De Operis Novi Nunciatione*.[37] If on my land I cut the source of water that feeds my neighbor's well to injure him, I am bound to repay the damage. But if I do this with no intent of fraud but only intending to look to my own utility, for instance, if I cannot conveniently build a wall I need without cutting off the streams that traverse my land, I do the other no injury, for I have the right to do what is useful to develop my land. As the *Rule of Ancient Law*[38] puts it: *"No one is considered to commit a fraud who does what he has a right to do."* But one has a right to procure a benefice for himself, provided he does so in a just and honorable way.

Endnotes; The English Translation

[1] In the *Ordinatio* IV, dist. 15, q. 1, n. 7 (15, 180) Scotus gives this definition of satisfaction: *"Satisfaction is the voluntary return of something equivalent that is otherwise not owed."* The first point, namely, it is a *return*, is evident, because it is not an absolute gift; for the very prefix "satis" (= enough) indicates it is commensurate with something corresponding that preceded it. That it is said to be *voluntary* is clear, because it it were involuntary it would not be satisfaction but sufficient punishment, and in this sense he, from whom due punishment in hell is demanded for the sin he committed, suffers enough, but does not make satisfaction. That it is also *equivalent* is evident, because this is already implied by the prefix "satis" or "enough". Justice also requires the return of satisfaction for that [offense] corresponding to it. The fourth point, namely, it is *otherwise not owed* is evident, because if it were otherwise owed [i.e., if it were an unjust possession of something due to another], it would not satisfy for this [offense], for it would not correspond in justice precisely to the offense, but to something else [that already belongs to another]."

[2] Scotus does not indicate just what sorts of satisfaction fall under this most general definition. In explaining in what sense theologians regard some personal acts of satisfaction on the part of the penitent as "the third part of penance," however, Scotus

shows the essential difference between such acts and those of restitution. Though satisfaction and restitution bear a superficial resemblance to one another in that both are an attempt to repair an injury done to another person, the rationale between them is quite different. "Satisfaction consists more in acts of punishment or of voluntary suffering than in other good actions that are not of a punitive nature" *Ibid.*, n. 8 (18, 198). Such acts of satisfaction whether internal, like sorrow or remorse or external like confession, fasting, almsgiving, etc. are all acts of supererogation. Acts of restitution, by contrast, are not supererogatory, but an attempt to restore to the injured party what is owed in strict justice.

[3] This work of Pelagius written to Pope Innocent in 417 A.D., from before the time of Charlesmagne throughout the Middle Ages was attributed to St. Jerome. Peter Lombard refers to this particular anathema of "Jerome" in Bk. II, dist. 36, n. 3 (cf. *Magistri Petri Lombardi Sententiae in IV libris distinctae* [Grottaferrata (Romae) Collegii S. Bonaventurae, 1971-1988, tom. I, p. 542].

[4] The original constitution *Romana ecclesia* by Innocent IV in the First Council of Lyons set forth the detailed canonical obligations of each archbishop to regularly visit the cities, dioceses, and cathedral chapters in his province. In addition, however, it forbad him to request or receive any money or special gifts over and above moderate necessary expenses for food, lodging, and travel, and if any had previously accepted such, he was to return double the amount. These general norms were also to govern the form of other canonical visitations, whether by bishops and other religious prelates visiting their subjects, except where approved constitutions for religious orders and regular institutes decreed otherwise. Because some canonical Visitors had come to expect or even had the audacity to demand monetary and other expensive gifts from the churches they visited, Gregory X in the Second Council of Lyons reiterated the demands of the original constitution of Innocent IV, requiring double restitution to the churches visited for such illegal gifts. If delayed beyond a month's time patriarchs, archbishops, and bishops incurred ipso facto interdict; lesser prelates were suspended from office or their benefice unless they returned such gifts to their respective donors. Boniface VIII, himself a canon lawyer by profession, collected these constitutions of his papal predecessors regarding canonical Visitors and added several of his own in his *Sixth Book of the Decretals.* Scotus apparently refers to these as the "New Constitutions."

[5] Here the loan is of something other than money; see the Introduction, p. 10 for the distinction between a fungible and non-fungible good..

[6] For reasons explained in the Introduction (pp. 10-11), the scholastics agreed that in accepting a money loan (*mutuum*) where money is being used as a medium of exchange there is a temporary transfer of ownership as well as use. Where money is loaned on bailment, however, the use of the money for its intrinsic value and not for exchange, as Scotus explains (p. 63), is simply a contract of renting or hiring. Note also that "accepting a money loan" or *mutuum* is different from entering in to a business partnership (*societas*) where the banker contributes the capital and the merchant the labor, and both share proportionately in risk and profit of their common enterprise. Though Scotus does not discuss *societas* , he does make a passing reference (p. 85) to a special type of business money loan where one accepts money from a banker (*pecunia foenebri*) and pays in return a legitimate fee to the financier or money lender (*foenerator*) for this service.

[7] As Wadding pointed out, in Scotus' Paris *Reportatio* IV, dist. 15, q. 4, n. 24 the reference reads "De hoc in tertio, in materia de usuries," but Scotus never treated this in Bk. III of the Oxford commentary, and in the Paris lectures he never reached distinction 37 where the Master [Peter Lombard] treats of this matter in the second part of that distinction. (See "Censura R.P.F. Lucae Waddingi" in the Wadding-Vivès edition, vol. 22, p. 2). This reference is one of several Scotus made in revising his *Ordinatio* to portions he intended to include, but never lived to dictate. This is understandable if he was still working on the latter portion of the *Ordinatio* after coming to Paris.

[8] The exceptions refer to the so-called 'extrinsic reasons' for accepting interest on money loans, because they are only incidentally connected with the notion of a loan. See *infra* note 12.

[9] John T. Noonan refers to this as the "thomistic argument" and apparently believed Scotus had Aquinas principally in mind. (*The Scholastic Analysis of Usury* [Cambridge: Harvard University Press, 1957], pp. 60-61) But Noonan can hardly be right. To begin with the argument is neither original nor peculiar to Aquinas, and Scotus clearly had some well known Franciscan in mind for he uses an argument based on the papal interpretation of the Franciscan rule which he would be forced to accept. The editors of the Wadding edition, therefore, seem to be quite justified in attributing this to Richard of Mediavilla, whom his mentor Magister Gonsalvus Hispanus so frequently quoted, the same "quidam Doctor" Scotus had referred to earlier (p. 54). Incidentally the editors were guided probably by the Scotist William Vorillon who wrote a special tract to identify the anonymous references Scotus made. See Richardus de Mediavilla, *Super quatuor libros Sententiarum Petri Lombardi Quaestiones subtilissimae*, lib. 4, dist. 25, art. 5, q. 5: "Utrum quilibet in aliquo contractu accipines aliquid ultra sortem teneatur ad restitutionem illius." (pp. 222-24) Richard's argument runs as follows: "*Ratio autem quare pro re mutuata nihil potest exigi ultra sortem*, et potest pro re locata est, *quia mutuus est de illis rebus, quarum principalis usus non potest concedi sine re ipsa*, eo quod ille usus est earum consumptio, sicut patet in edibilibus et potabilibus, vel distractio, ut patet in pecunia, quae ad hoc principaliter inventa est, ut expendatur in emptione aliarum rerum, et propter hoc cum tales res aliis conceduntur, transfertur in illos earum dominium, unde mutuare est de meo tuum facere, cum ergo concedere principalem usum talium rerum fit concedere res ipsas, ille qui ultra recompensationem rei exigit recompensationem pro usu exigit pro eadem recompensationem bis, aut recompensationem pro eo quod non est, quod est contra aequalitatem iuris naturalis" (ed. Brixiae, 1591), tom. IV, p. 223).

[10] See the Introduction, p. 11.

[11] A more literal translation would be: "This is what the word means: By a *mutuum* [or *mine/yours*] I give to you what is mine." In the original *Reportatio* IV A, however, Scotus makes this play on words even clearer; there he says: "As the very sound of the name *mutuum* tells us, one transfers to another the ownership of the thing together with its use, by making mine yours, and his another's." [Sicut sonat nomen mutui, simul cum usu rei transfert dominium rei in alium, *faciendo de meo tuum*, et de suo alienum.] Vivès ed., vol. 24, p.240.

[12] See the notion of usury in the Introduction, pp. 9-12. In a usurious loan, the borrower pays a surcharge for using the money; here he pays it as insurance against a possible damage to the lender for delaying or failing to return the money on time. It is

never licit to charge for the money loan itself, but it always lawful to protect oneself from possible damage. The penalty is payed only if the borrower defaults on his contract. Scotus later on (p. 85) makes passing reference to "requisite profit" (*lucrum requisitum*) a professional money lender or banker can claim. He seems to be referring here to *foenum* or business money loan; the *mutuum* according to Roman law is a gratuitous contract unless turned into a *foenum* by a stipulation or formal promise regarding the special conditions of repayment. In such a business loan there has to be a requisite profit to the banker, just as there is profit to the financial backer in the *societas* or business partnership.

[13] Interest, as we said in the Introduction, (p. 9) refers to compensation for a loss due to a failure to repay the loan on time and is never regarded as the price payed for a loan. Derived from "inter est," *interesse* (interest) expresses the "difference between" the injured party's present position and what it would have been had borrower lived up to the obligation of his contract. Roman jurists apply the term *quod interest* to various damage claims, and only incidentally to one involving a money loan. *Usura* (meaning "use" or "enjoyment") is their technical term for the price of a loan or for any money payment beyond the principal. The early canonists and theologians took over these technical terms from Roman law.

[14] This is the famous *venditio sub dubio* (see Noonan, *op. cit.*, pp. 90-95). The uncertainity or doubt has to do with whether the market price of commodities will change in the future and whether by selling earlier one may insure oneself against a posssible loss or by charging more than the present fair market price one may guarantee oneself a profit on future deliveries. The intention to profit on a sale is always licit, but the intention to profit on a loan as such is illicit. The canonists who appeal to the decretals Scotus refers to explicity exclude money as being an object of a *venditio sub dubio*. Though it is not a commodity and is regarded as having a fixed face-value by law, money as a medium of exchange can enter in to contracts involving sales where the value of what is bought or sold varies with the passing of time.

[15] The *Naviganti* of Gregory IX, as Noonan notes, "is the most important single papal decree on the usury question with the exception of those containing the basic prohibition itself. It has the paradoxical distinction of containing in two sentences the seemingly most severe and the seemingly most liberal interpretations of the usury law ever put out by papal authority" (*op. cit.*, p. 137). It contains three distinct decrees. The first reads 'One lending a certain quantity of money to one sailing or going to a fair, in order to receive something beyond the capital for this that he takes upon himself the peril, is to be thought a usurer.' This seems to be primarily a condemnation of the sea-loan where the lender took upon himself to cover completely any loss that occurred at sea, but charged the borrower twice the amount for such insurance. The same would hold good where the money lender insures any loss that occurs during the journey to the fair. The other two decrees concern the *venditio sub dubio*. The first states that a discount for the anticipated payment was not usurious if there was a real doubt at the time of payment as to what the value of the merchandise would be at the time of delivery. The second of these, referred to by Scotus as *Ratione*, is the converse case of charging a higher price for credit sales where there is a doubt as to the future value. This is a reaffirmation of Alexander III's permission *In civitate tua*, but Gregory adds a condition that the seller must not have intended to sell on credit, but originally planned to market the goods at the later cash price. It reads in

translation: "By reason of this doubt he is also excused, who sells cloth, grain, wine, oil or other merchandise that he may receive for these after a certain period more than they are now worth; provided at the time of the contract he had not been about to sell."

[16] According to the wording, this paragraph refers specifically to this third condition and it should be included as part of it. The editors of the Wadding edition, however, singled it out as a major subdivision. Note, however, that the second condition of accepting interest in the case of actual damage is also licit, even if there is no pact; the first condition of an added penalty for default on the contract and hence possible damage, however, seems of its nature to involve some kind of an explicit pact.

[17] These two rules are Scotus' version of how to reconcile the papal declarations regarding the prohibition of usury and the condemnation of higher prices for credit sales on the one hand and papal execeptions based on the right to charge a just price for merchandise that may change in value on the other. On how other scholastics of Scotus' day walked the tightrope between the usury prohibitions and the concept of a just price, see Noonan, *op. cit.*, pp. 89-99.

[18] This decretal to which Scotus refers is taken from a letter of Pope Urban III which declares flatly that a credit sale for a much higher price than the current cash one is usury. As Noonan points out: "The immense importance of this decree can hardly be exaggerated. Here for the first time in the entire tradition, a specific command of Christ is authoritatively interpreted by a pope as probiting usury. Henceforth, effectively unquestioned till Dominic Soto in the sixteenth century, Luke 6:35 will stand as an absolute divine prohibition of gain from a loan. Moreover, not only is the papal reference of the highest interest in itself, but the use made of it by Urban is of equal importance. He has been called on to decide two cases in which it is question whether usury is present. In one no contractual stipulation for usury has been made, but the lender would not lend without hope of gain; the other is the old case of sales as a higher price on credit. Urban decides both by the criterion of intention. The lender in each case intends to receive gain from a loan; this is prohibited by Luke 6:35; the lenders are therefore guilty of moral usurty. Again and again, scholastics writers will recur to this biblical text and to the Pope's application of it to show that the intention to gain will alone constitute usury" (*op. cit.*, p. 20).

[19] Confer note 15 supra.

[20] The reference is to *In civitate tua*, of Alexander III, contained in the *Decretales Gregorii IX*, lib. V, titulus 19, cap. 6; *Corpus Iuris Canonici*, II, col. 813. The intention of Alexander III was to close a loophole used by usurers to charge more for credit sales even though the explicit form of the contract is not that of a loan. "In your city it frequently happens that when certain ones purchase pepper or cinnamon or other wares, which are then not valued over five pounds, they promise in a publically recorded document to pay six pounds to those from whom they received these wares after a stated time. But even though such contracts as are in a form of this sort cannot be censured under the name of usury, nevertheless their vendors commit sin, unless there is doubt that those wares will have more or less that value at the time of payment. And therefore the citizens are well advised by your excellency to desist from such contracts since the thoughts of men are not hidden from an omnipotent God."

[21] Though Alexander III in admitting the exception that payments should not be considered usurious if there is a real doubt at the time of the sale as to the future value of the merchandise, the Pope counseled against charging more even in such a case. Scotus quotes Alexander's exception not in the form given it by that pope, but as reaffirmed by Gregory IX in *Naviganti*, where this counsel is omitted. Hence Scotus is correct is declaring one is doing a favor if one does what Alexander advised.

[22] Scotus referred above (note 4) to this canon forbidding canonical visitors pressuring the churches or communities visited to give some monetary "gift" on the occasion of the visitation. Here he cites it as a proof that donations must be freely given.

[23] This canon of Innocent III had to do with proper clerical dress and behavior. Among other things it forbad clerics attending public gambling houses. Scotus is concerned with their obligation of restitution of ill-gotten gains.

[24] This decretal is from a letter of Pope Alexander III to Archbishop Panormitanus declaring that Church cannot dispense from the prohibition against usury, even to raise money for ransoming Christian captives from the Saracens, for usury is "a crime destested by the pages of both Testaments."

[25] As Noonan notes this argument which goes back to William of Auxerre (1160 - 1299) will become the standard argument against higher prices for credit sales (*op. cit.*, p. 44).

[26] *De congruo* is contrasted with *de condigno*. Theologians use the terms to distinguish in what sense a creature can make satisfaction to God for sin. Adequate satisfaction would *de condigno*. But a sinful creature can perform no act in such a state that would measure up such a degree of satisfaction. But through the sacrament of penance a creature can make an appropriate or *de conguo* response that would serve to satisfy God for the offense committed against him.

[27] As Anthony Hickey explains in his commentary, Scotus is making a double point here: "Here he has distinguished between the natural fruit and that due to one's industry; and the rule he hands down is most certain and common, namely to be held to the restitution both of the thing and the fruit it bears of itself, after expenses are subtracted, if some improvement or industry was employed. Also the other part of the rule is that there is no obligation of restoring the fruit acquired by one's own industry, as when the thing is not something that bears fruit of itself, for example, the money of the money lender, which the usurer expends through just negotiation, and is rewarded for his industry by something over and above the capital. See the proof of this in the text" (*Joannis Duns Scoti opera omnia*, Wadding-Vivès, vol. 18, 333b).

[28] Reference to this remark of Scotus was made *supra* in notes 6 and 12. Scotus' terminology suggests he is referring to a business loan or *foenum* rather than a formal partnership or *societas* recognized by Roman law and accepted as legitimate by the scholastic theologians since the twelfth century. The acceptance of risk was the classical reason given for distinguishing such a legitimate business arrangement from a usurious loan where the debitor bore all the risk. For it is obvious that the usury prohibitions by the Church were not meant to eliminate the need for legitimate bankers or money lenders to finance merchants willing to contribute the work but without capital of their own. The point the Church made however was that that they are not selling time, nor is money fertile of itself, but it is the industry of the capitalist in acquiring his capital and putting it

into profitable investments that is rewarded by a modest return. Since Scotus, like Giles of Rome, never refers explicitly to the *societas*, it may well be that in his day no sharp distinction was made between *societas* and *foenum* where the surcharge was minimal and corresponded to the industry of the investor. This would also explain what appears to be an incidental remark on his part, namely that the fact that a money lender is entitled to some profit as the fruit of his industry provides a great incentive for him to practice usury.

[29] This seems to be a reference to the use of the capital originally owned by the banker or financier but no longer his property during the duration of a business loan.

[30] This decree of Pope Gregory IX decided that a cleric who could not pay his creditors without great difficulty ought not to be excommunicated or otherwise molested, provided he swear that he will pay when he comes into more fortunate circumstances.

[31] It would seem that lost articles could be claimed either by the finder or given to the poor or auctioned, according to the custom or laws regarding lost property.

[32] Pope Nicholas III mentions this basic principle in the papal bull *Exiit qui seminat* explaining the Rule of the Friars Minor (Franciscans). As Scotus indicates it was incorporated by Pope Boniface VIII, himself a canonist, in Bk. VI of Canon Law. The significant words of Nicholas III read in translation: "Friars, like anybody else, would still have open to them in the pinch of extreme need the so-called right of existence, to provide for their natural sustenance, a way conceded to everybody in the grip of extreme need, since extreme need is exempt from any law."

[33] See the note 30 *supra*.

[34] Both MSS incorrectly refer to this as the third article; the Wadding-Vivès edition correctly cites it as we have translated it here.

[35] See note 30 above.

[36] It seems Scotus intended to add an eighth argument about unjustly acquiring a benefice to the seven listed in the initial Pro and Con. Codex A suggests Scotus neglected to do this by the marginal note: "Istud non est supra argutum." The argument is found in the parallel text of the Paris *Reportatio* (IV, dist. 15, q. 2) in this form: "Item aliquis potest beneficium alteri conferendum sibi efficaciter procurare, et procurando sibi ab alio auferre, et tamen non tenetur beneficium sibi procuratum illi restituere; igitur" (Wadding-Vivès, vol. 25, 232). "Also, someone can efficaciously procure for himself a benefice conferred on another, and by so doing, he would be taking it away from another; and nevertheless he is not bound to restore the benefice to the other; therefore, etc." Wadding inserts a similar text in his version of the *Opus oxoniense*, but leaves out the fact that the benefice was already "conferred on another" (alteri conferendum) as well as it was "efficaciously" (efficaciter) procured. Scotus seems to be answering both possibilities, viz. that the benefice may or may not have been unjustly procured.

[37] Scotus quotes the first title (On the Notice of a New Work) of the Book 39 of Justinian's *Digest or Pandects*. The second law he is referring to, however, is under the third title "On Water and the Diversion of Rain Water" (title 3, n. 12: "When anyone while excavating upon his own land, diverts a vein of water belonging to his neighbor, no action can be brought against him, not even on the grounds of malice. And it is evident that he should not have such a right of action, where his neighbor did not intend to injure him, but did the work for the purpose of improving his own property." See *Corpus Iuris Civilis*

(ed. P Krueger. Berlin: Apud Weidmannos, 1954, reprint Dublin/Zurick 1970), vol. I, p. 645.

[38] *Digest*, lib. 50, tit. 17, n. 151: De diversis regulis Juris: *"Nemo damnum facit nisi qui illud facit, quod facere jus non habet." Corpus Iuris Civilis* I, p. 924.